Your Innovator Brain

The Truth About ADHD

Carol Gignoux

BALBOA.
PRESS
A DIVISION OF HAY HOUSE

Balboa Press books may be ordered through booksellers or by contacting:

Balboa Press
A Division of Hay House
1663 Liberty Drive
Bloomington, IN 47403
www.balboapress.com
1 (877) 407-4847

Print information available on the last page.

ISBN: 978-1-5043-4583-5 (sc)
ISBN: 978-1-5043-4585-9 (hc)
ISBN: 978-1-5043-4584-2 (e)

Library of Congress Control Number: 2015919097

Balboa Press rev. date: 04/07/2016

To my daughter, Molly, who is courageous, funny, and smart and who has an unwavering devotion to her family. And to my son, Matthew, whose spirit, intelligence, and wry sense of humor are sorely missed.

And to my clients, past and present, who trusted me to help them on their journeys to find their gifts. I learned a lot from them, and I am eternally grateful for their guidance.

CONTENTS

In closing, I remind all of us not to let the pain of the past hold us back from the possibilities of the future. I believe that in particular those with the innovator brain type have valuable contributions to offer their families, their communities, art, science, medicine, technology, and the world economy. Innovator brain thinkers should be supported and not hindered so that their innovative ideas and concepts can make the world a better place.

PART 1

From ADHD to the Innovator Brain

This book is unlike any you have ever read about what is commonly referred to as attention-deficit/hyperactivity disorder or ADHD. I wrote it not only with the specific intention and hope that it would be a game changer but also out of profound compassion and respect for the millions of people who have been diagnosed with, treat, teach, counsel, or have family, friends, or partners with ADHD.

Constantly shifting between multiple name changes and agreement on symptomology, I believe that the psychiatric field has never handled ADHD adequately or fairly. Historically this categorization or label has dwelled too much on the behavioral side effects of ADHD rather than looking closely at its fascinating cause, namely a brain with faster processing speeds. A diagnosis of ADHD is in fact only one aspect of what I would call a brain type, specifically the innovator brain.

This book argues that the current pathology-focused and one-dimensional label of ADHD obscures our full recognition and appreciation of the complex and whole individuals who possess innovator brains. I invite you to consider that we can understand the gifts and challenges of ADHD more holistically when it is approached from the perspective of a brain type as opposed to a narrow disorder or disability. Men and women with ADHD, both past and present, are arguably some of the most brilliant, inspired, and creative people who have walked the earth. However, few of us would recognize them for their ADHD disorder but rather for the genius derived from the blessing of an innovator brain. Here are just a few of these highly original individuals who employed their fast-processing brains toward magnificent ends: Pablo Picasso, Leo Tolstoy, Robert Frost, Ludwig van Beethoven, Charlie Chaplin, Whoopi Goldberg, John Lennon, Henry Ford, Isaac Newton, Jonas Salk, Carl Jung, Nelson Rockefeller, Walt Disney, Dwight Eisenhower, and Steve Jobs.

Part 1 of this book begins by examining the current problematic definition of ADHD and its implications for patients and the professionals supporting them. This section then goes on to juxtapose traditional approaches to ADHD with the very different approach of understanding and harnessing the gifts and challenges of the innovator brain type.

Chapter 1 explores typical approaches to the treatment and understanding of ADHD concentrated on disability and disorder. Currently it is generally accepted that the ADHD brain is neurologically impaired and that little can be done to improve it as a result. Medication may help someone focus better, but essentially the die is cast. However, I have worked for almost forty years with hundreds of clients of diverse ages and backgrounds, and I have had a dramatically different experience of supporting people with ADHD. It is based on this experience that I offer my alternative approach to ADHD, providing a user's guide for the innovator brain.

I want to be clear that I am not saying that people with innovator brains are entirely free of behavior management issues. Lack of necessary behavior controls and the consequences of not sufficiently balancing one's gifts and challenges is after all the reason people were labeled ADHD in the first place. Instead I am suggesting that the unique approach and support of this guide as opposed to the more traditional ways of treating ADHD. My protocol helps people with magnificent innovator brains learn to tap into their brains' amazing resources so that their achievements outshine their behavioral limitations.

Everyone diagnosed with ADHD has been confronted by its ugly stigma. In chapter 2, I address this burden head-on, empowering my readers to redefine the expectations placed on them by society and themselves. Finally in chapter 3, I discuss my personal and professional journey spanning four decades from being an ADHD child (then called "minimal brain dysfunction") to becoming a successful business owner, coach, and speaker on the cutting edge of the ADHD industry.

I look forward to beginning this journey with you!

CHAPTER 1

Redefining ADHD: The Innovator Brain

Constantly shifting between multiple name changes and symptom definitions, the psychiatric field has never handled ADD/ADHD adequately or fairly. The fifth edition of *The Diagnostic and Statistical Manual of Mental Disorders* (DSM-5) of the American Psychiatric Association defines ADHD as follows: "A neurodevelopmental disorder defined by impairing levels of inattention, disorganization, and/or hyperactivity-impulsivity." Let's take a close look at this. *Inattention* and *disorganization* refer to the ability to stay on task. *Disorganization* can also take the form of not listening and losing or misplacing materials at levels that are inconsistent with age or developmental level. *Hyperactivity/impulsivity* entails overactivity, fidgeting, not able to stay seated, intruding into other people's activities and inability to wait excessive for developmental age. That is why hyperactive children tend to get identified early on and those children who do not have the H in ADHD fly under the radar a bit longer. These children and adults tend to daydream and seem off in their own world (Griffin, 2014).

We will be talking more about symptoms and identifying features of ADHD as we go along. But first I want to make the case for why the profession of psychiatry has been guilty of unfairly pathologizing an entire segment of the population and would do well to reflect on the outcome of their assumptions and practices.

Disorder and Disability

But what really is ADHD? For decades people ranging from neurologists to psychologists to psychiatrists have not been able to agree. Is it really a disability and a disorder? When people believe they have a disorder, they often develop tendency to give less effort to achieve and better themselves, and they may have tried hard if they had only felt more capable. When people are told they have a disability, they are more likely to accept that they cannot overcome being disabled, and accepting this fate can become a self-fulfilling prophecy for them. Adults may fall into thinking and behaving patterns that fall short of their own expectations, patterns like giving up on trying to excel at work or on trying to communicate better with their wives or husbands. Children tend to suffer in silence and to avoid the possibility of appearing stupid and clueless in front of teachers and classmates, so they hold back from interacting. What if having this brain type meant seeing and doing things differently? What if having a rapid-firing brain wasn't all about disadvantages without advantages? Suppose people with ADHD were not forced to settle for a lifetime of disorganization, lack of planning, and poor communication? These are the questions we will be discussing as we continue to explore the truth about this brain type.

Typical approaches to the treatment and understanding of ADHD concentrate on disability and disorder. The people identified or diagnosed are seen as being permanently less capable and competent than they would have been without their disabilities. Therefore, they must adapt to lives of struggling to do the best they can in spite of serious shortcomings. Above all, they must not get their hopes up that it will be possible for them to overcome their challenges. Since the ADHD brain is neurologically "impaired" (versus wired differently as I have come to understand), medication has been used to help people achieve better focus. Traditionally the only help individuals could get for the lack of life-management skills fell into the following categories: diagnosis, medication, and therapy. However, none of these approaches addresses people's needs to build confidence in themselves through understanding how their brains operate. Medication may help people slow down and focus better, and therapy may help them cope with depression or anxiety disorders. But where is the help—and hope—that a person with this brain type can successfully fit into society and live up to expectations of others? Traditional approaches assume these people need to be fixed. Typical recommendations require people take pills and learn to accept and live with their disabilities through therapy. They are advised to lower their expectations regarding the success and productivity they can achieve. To me this has always sounded like they must resign themselves to their fates. The die is cast. I believe this cannot be further from the truth. Next I will explain how my approach and assumptions are completely different from current treatment methods and assumptions.

I have worked for almost forty years with hundreds of clients of differing ages, and I have had a dramatically different experience. I have seen people with this brain type display considerable strengths and talents when given the tools and the confidence. In my experience the people diagnosed as ADHD (when exposed to the protocol I have developed) come across more as gifted innovators than mentally and behaviorally challenged misfits. From my well-honed perspective, categorizing and labeling people with ADHD or attention deficit disorder is responsible for reinforcing weaknesses and promoting negative attitudes and perspectives both on the part of the person being identified and those with whom he or she interacts. This diagnosis becomes a self-fulfilling prophecy that in turn justifies the label ADHD. Yet I have witnessed people over and over again break free of the ADHD stereotype after they see themselves from a gifted and talented perspective. They were able to gain a new vision for their lives, realize their true abilities, and embrace the confidence to succeed.

From ADHD Disorder to the Innovator Brain

In moving away from ADHD label, I will explain how I came up with the new label of innovator to describe this brain type. I will explain how ADHD really does mean innovation by using historical and contemporary examples of people, their accomplishments, and their struggles. It is critical to understand why we are wrong about the label ADD or ADHD to describe this brain type. It is important to remember that if we continue to define people by using a label that makes them feel less capable than others, they will struggle to believe in their abilities to overcome their challenges.

The label attention deficit disorder (ADD) or attention-deficit/hyperactivity disorder (ADHD) assumes that the brain type is a disorder and a disability. This definition comes directly from the profession of psychiatry and their diagnostic and statistical manual. Psychiatry makes decisions about a person's mental and emotional functioning according to certain precepts of what it believes constitutes mental health and what it believes constitutes mental illness. By assuming that people with ADHD are dysfunctional, the profession of psychiatry is essentially telling them that addressing their issues and improving their lives is unobtainable. If you feel that your brain is not organically equipped to change patterns of unsuitable behavior, why would you try? People with ADHD are thought to have a deficit of attention, and yet it seems to make more sense that they have a surplus of attention from their rapid-firing brains rather than a deficit. Can this brain type be a disorder when people who fall within this spectrum lead successful albeit frustrating lives, often contributing to advancements in science, medicine, and the arts, making a difference in the lives of others with compassion and understanding? There is a strong history of extraordinary world leaders, inventors, scientists, and problem solvers with the same brain type. Psychiatry describes ADHD as a neurological condition caused by lower-than-normal levels of the chemical dopamine. Since dopamine is responsible for inhibiting certain impulses in the brain, lower levels could cause a disruption in the pathways of the brain that affect behavior and motivation. However, in people described as ADHD, behaviors manifest themselves in different ways. What may be a type of strength for some could be a weakness for others. Even within the same person, impulsivity could be the best strategy for finding an immediate and effective solution to a looming problem and the worse strategy for coming to a decision after a long and laborious process. Additionally, what is motivating for one person could be challenging for another. After all, they are different people.

In order for all of us to be on the same page from now on, we need to address the truth about ADHD. Is it a disorder, or is it more aptly referred to as the super evolved gene, a rapid-firing brain, Edison gene, Einstein gene, or innovator brain? After decades of research and direct work with people, what I have found to be most true about this brain type and what seems to have the best fit is the title *innovator brain*. After forty years of work with people who live with this brain type, I have found this title to be the most fitting. As you will notice in chapter 1, we will still use ADHD to point out the deficiencies in the label and as a way of transitioning you, the reader, to the new title of innovator brain. By the time we get to chapter 2, we will begin to use the innovator brain type, or some version of that description, exclusively when we refer to the power of this amazing brain. In a general sense, an innovator is a person who is one of the first to introduce into reality something better than before and to open up a new area for others to participate in. The strengths of people with the so-called ADHD brain fit that definition better than any other definition I have been able to come up with in my forty years in the field. Having researched and studied the many innovators in the world, past and present, they also seem to have much in common with the ADHD brain type.

I know that many people reading this book will be able to relate to this description of how it feels to grow up ADHD because the stories are similar from person to person. ADHD follows a very recognizable path with anticipated consequences. This is an important question to ask. Why do we pretend to not understand people with the ADHD brain type when we already know so much about how they operate? Wouldn't our time and money be better spent on coming up with a way to teach and train people to manage their ADHD challenges? I believe the answer is yes, and that is why I have worked for decades to understand and find the best practices to help people feel competent, smart, and capable of managing their lives. I help them understand how they are capable of making important contributions as a result of having the ADHD brain, not in spite of having it.

History

ADHD has been called the "hidden disability" because it does not appear as a disability at all. People look normal but behave badly. They don't seem to care about themselves or others, and they do the most annoying things that frustrate us to no end. Society historically has had little compassion for people who display ADHD characteristics. As a result, people with ADHD have had no compassion for themselves. Instead of the confidence to advocate for what they needed and the belief they could obtain it, the hopes and aspirations of those labeled ADHD have been allowed to whither on the vine and fade from sight. Instead of fighting for the right to be accepted for who they are, many people with this brain type have given up their rights to have the understanding and help they need, and along with it, they have surrendered their dreams and fighting spirits. I believe that the day for blame is over and that the day for celebration is near.

If you have been labeled ADHD and have suffered with a lack of help and a lack of understanding, it is likely you did the best you could do under the circumstances. The right kind of help can still be difficult to find. Until recently and still in certain locations in this country and around the world, ADHD coaching—a type of intervention we have found to be highly effective in helping people bring their behaviors under control—is either unknown or unavailable. During our journey we will be exploring the many ways that people with a knack for superb creative talent and problem-solving abilities—mistakenly referred as ADHD or disabled and disordered—can be given the tools to bring their gifts to the world by way of the help of a professional ADHD coach.

I'm going to walk you through an exercise now that will help you compare and contrast traditional beliefs and perceptions about this brain type with my own. I have created this first list as a compilation of the things I hear people complain about and say they believe about ADHD and the way it manifests itself. Some of them you may agree with, and some of them you may disagree agree with.

- It is inherited from one or both parents.
- People with ADHD are good at compensating for their differences until demands become too high.
- Common symptoms are distractibility, impulsivity, disorganization, and a rapid-firing brain.
- People with the ADHD brain can become easily overwhelmed and thrown off course.
- It is a brain type that is primarily characterized by living in the moment without thinking about the future.
- There is a tendency to think of all activities or tasks as equal in importance.

- There are often accompanying conditions such as anxiety, depression, obsessive-compulsive disorder, and bipolar disorder.
- People with ADHD often feel disappointed in themselves and less worthy as compared to others.
- Those who have this brain type often grow up feeling like they don't fit in.
- There is a reluctance to draw attention to oneself for fear of appearing stupid.
- People with ADHD often jangle our nerves.

While we are looking at the ADHD behaviors people complain about, we need to also look at the ADHD behaviors that serve individuals well and make it possible for them to do outstanding work and make exceptional contributions. If we don't admit this list exists and has validity, we continue to reinforce the stigma of disorder and disability by preventing people with this brain type from having confidence and hope. We knowingly inhibit their chances of living better and having worthwhile lives. My experience with the hundreds of people with ADHD I have worked with through the years has shown me that living with the stigma can take a toll in job performance, personal relationships, and self-worth.

This list will help you look candidly at what neuroscience, psychology, and ADHD coaching are discovering that changes our present understanding of the ADHD brain. Here is my list of the upside of having an ADHD brain:

- They have insatiable curiosity.
- They exhibit a higher level of creativity when it comes to solving both large and small problems.
- They have the ability to be exceptionally inventive in response to the needs around them.
- Their innovation skills are way above average and extraordinary.

- They have a natural inclination to follow their instincts and use out-of-the-box thinking
- They are often living in the moment, jumping from possibility to possibility, and finding clues.
- They follow clues to their natural conclusions.
- They have a basic sense of compassion and care for others and the problems around them.
- They have a nonlinear sense of things that helps them identify solutions more quickly.
- They dig in and "hyper focus" on something to the exclusion of everything else.
- Historically they have constituted our greatest innovators and problem solvers.

Early on while I was working with people who fit the description of this brain type, I discovered that impulsivity in one area could be considered inappropriate while impulsivity in another area could be considered good problem solving. For example, when it is necessary to follow a routine to ensure a task is completed on time, being impulsive and switching focus to other topics would likely get in the way. But when a cure for cancer is being explored, the greater the level of impulsivity, the more likely the researcher is to apply better and better methods of finding one. This is also true for disorganization. While managing a portfolio of someone's wealth requires a high level of organization, as any portfolio manager would tell you, the same portfolio manager would also say impulsivity is a good thing when one is searching and exploring better financial options. I cannot imagine Picasso inventing cubism had he not had impulsivity on his side as a welcome strategy. I help my clients embrace all of their behaviors despite what they have grown up to believe or the feedback they have gotten from others. Instead they learn to make the right distinctions between the proper and improper time to be impulsive or focused, organized or intuitive, attending to the needs of others or attending to the needs of themselves. My clients tell me that it is good news to know that they are not broken and that they don't need to be fixed. They are relieved to know that improving their behaviors, their relationships, and their abilities to communicate is something they can learn to change with practice, understanding, and the right professionals to support them.

A Better Description

So how do we justify the upside and so-called downside of the ADHD brain type?

This is an exciting moment for me because for so long I have not only been vehemently opposed to the label ADHD but also have continually felt a grave injustice was being done to people with the innovator brain. Most importantly, it is a great relief to move away from deficit disordered to innovative problem solver. With that decision, we can begin to help people with this brain type learn to manage their behaviors from a place of confidence and self-esteem. From now on in this book, you will notice a striking difference between what people are actually able to accomplish in terms of behavior change when they consider themselves innovative problem solvers as opposed to times when they think of themselves as deficit-disordered misfits. So remember to replace ADHD with innovator gene, innovator brain, or innovator problem solver as we go along. You'll get used to it pretty quickly, and I believe you'll even begin to approve of the change.

New Approaches to Managing ADHD: User's Guide to Your Innovator Brain

Have you noticed like I have that there always seems to be less talk about the highly valuable assets that are part of this brain type and more talk about the difficulties? Society tends to believe so strongly in the difficulties that its members tend to tune out the plusses. As a result of focusing on the negatives, the positives are forgotten or lost along with the possibility that the positives could outweigh the negatives. It is no wonder that people with this fast-paced brain type tend to lose faith in themselves. Let's ask the question again. Can people with ADHD learn to sufficiently improve inattention and impulsivity with or without medication, or are they a prisoner forever to the outcomes of these behaviors?

Fortunately for everyone, those with and those without the innovator brain type, the answer is yes. Yes, a person labeled ADHD can learn to better fit into the expectations of the society around him or her. Yes, a person with this brain type can think ahead and plan ahead about how he or she will respond to cues in his or her environment. Through methodologies like professional coaching and cognitive behavioral therapy (CBT), with or without medication, people labeled ADHD need never be a prisoner to unwanted responses.

A way of looking at this is that we're all in this together. Your barber, bus driver, aunt, son, and financial advisor may be rapid-fire thinkers. You may be a rapid-fire thinker. When you walk into Google, MIT, or Caltech, how many people would fit the negative ADD profile? Obviously hundreds of thousands of members of the human family are born with the resource of rapid-fire thinking. What if it was up to us to understand, accept, and teach these diamonds in the rough?

Innovator Brain:?

It's not impossible for people who are rapid-fire thinkers to learn to live full lives with less anxiety and be powerful contributors to their families, communities, and societies. I know this from my own life and the lives of others with the innovator brain (or ADHD).

Shouldn't it be a crime to shut down potentially high-performing people because their behavior patterns jangle our nerves?

Shutting down is a term for a common occurrence among those who share this brain type. Have you ever noticed how someone can suddenly check out with no warning in the middle of a conversation? What about that person who doesn't answer your e-mails or phone calls and avoids interacting with you without warning? These are some examples of shutting-down behavior. It is unfortunately a last-ditch effort to save yourself from further pain, feelings of incompetence, and the feeling that you are a disappointment to others. The person in shutting-down mode closes off further input from the outside world and lives in a safer inner world of his or her own creation. This focus away from the painful moment distracts people from the reality they perceive as failure. It can take many forms, ranging from surfing the Internet to the exclusion of everything else or playing video games in a way that blots out all input from outside to self-medicating with marijuana, alcohol, or more serious substances like cocaine, pain pills, and opiates.

What if we could help more innovative thinkers avoid a tendency to shut down and work to understand and overcome other unwanted patterns of behavior? What innovative solutions to the many problems around us might we have as a result of encouraging more innovative thinkers to stand up for themselves? Rapid-fire thinkers are gifted and want to change the world. Einstein, Edison, Mozart, da Vinci—all could be annoying and were known to have issues with communication and relationships. Should they have been silenced?

There are many personalities, historical and contemporary, with the innovator gene, and they have made significant contributions. These highly original individuals used nonlinear thought processes that employed their intuitions as well as their intellects and more linear cognitive processes. Unfortunately many problem solvers do not either know they are or want to disclose they are innovators because of the stigma they feel society will apply to them.

As I mentioned in the introduction, we all know many accomplished and rather famous innovators throughout history. Some of our more contemporary innovator brain folks include Steve Jobs, Paul Neeleman of Jet Blue, Paul Orfalea of Kinkos, Jim Carrey, Ty Pennington, Sir Richard Branson, Justin Timberlake, Cameron Diaz, James Carville, among others.

This is only a partial list of the accomplished people we know about because they became famous for their game-changing contributions. What about the many people among us who are also very good at what they do—our many unsung heroes?

Other writers and contributors who echo my belief in the potential and valuable assets of people misnamed ADHD include Bryan Hutchinson (who has published such best-selling books as *One Boy's Struggle: Surviving Life with Undiagnosed ADD, The Brilliant Reality of ADHD*, and *Adult ADHD Can Be Sexy*) believes in the power of people with this brain type to overcome and succeed beyond their wildest dreams. Professor Michael Fitzgerald of Trinity College in Dublin in his article titled "Is ADHD a positive force for writers and others?" writes that risk taking can have its advantages and lead to breakthroughs in science, the arts, and exploration. He also writes that being able to hyper-focus in a narrow area of interest can foster creative genius (Wolff, 2010). Dr. Dale Archer, psychiatrist, in his article in *Forbes* magazine titled "ADHD: The Entrepreneur's Superpower," makes a case for entrepreneurs being successful because of their diagnoses rather than in spite of them. He cites business mogul Sir Richard Branson, Ikea founder Ingvar Kamprad, and Jet Blue founder David Neeleman, all of whom have an ADHD diagnosis in common (Archer, 2014). In his article "Top Ten Advantages of ADHD in a High Tech Career," nationally well-known ADHD coach Pete Quily lists the ability to multitask, hyper-focus, take risks, maintain high energy and creativity, learn quickly, seek stimulation, constantly scan environment, and act well in a crisis as perfect qualities for the job (Quily, 2006).

In his recent well-received book titled *The Innovators: How a Group of Hackers, Geniuses, and Geeks Created the Digital Revolution,* Walter Isaacson talks about the "talents that allowed certain innovators and entrepreneurs to turn their visionary ideas into disruptive realities" (Isaacson, 2015). A look through the innovators at the beginning of the book and their unique talents reads like a list of people with the same innovator brain type we have been talking about. And even though only a couple of women are mentioned in his time line as noteworthy, the very first person in the lineup was a woman by the name of Augusta Ada King, Countess of Lovelace. A British mathematician and writer, her notes on Charles Babbage's early mechanical general purpose computer included what is recognized as the first algorithm intended to be carried out by a machine. Frequently recognized as the very first computer programmer, could she be the mother of the digital revolution? (Wikipedia 2015)

Conclusion

In preparation for my groundbreaking theory and the rest of this book, we have discussed the accuracy and challenges of using the title ADHD to refer to people with a type characterized by a rapid-firing, sometimes impulsive, and often disorganized brain. We have questioned whether the profession of psychiatry has been accurate and fair with its characterization of this brain type as a disorder and a disability in the diagnostic and statistical manual DSM-5, the bible for this group. We have pointed out what we know to be true about this very same fascinating brain that has been associated with great thinkers, artists, and innovators of the past and present. We have noted what is commonly referred to as the downside and the upside of behaviors associated with the ADHD label.

We believe that understanding society's agreed-upon characterization of ADHD according to the profession of psychiatry is necessary in order to ask some important questions. How does their theory serve the people who they are supposed to be helping? Could there be a title given to this brain type and an explanation for it that affirms the capability of people rather than disables them? Could this new title and characterization be more accurate? And most importantly of all, could a new understanding that focuses on the strengths and gifts of the innovator brain be more helpful to those who are struggling? These are the questions we will be answering in this book. We hope the answers will bring relief to the millions of people who are needlessly suffering.

In chapter 2, we will begin to reconcile the confusion and disparities between psychiatry's formal diagnosis of ADHD with its disorder theory and real-life, observable evidence of this brain type through the use of the innovator brain type theory. We will begin chapter 2 by taking a look at the stigma associated with being labeled ADHD and its affect upon the lives of millions of people ranging from children to adults.

CHAPTER 2

Rejecting the Stigma

According to Peter Byrne, senior lecturer of the Kent Institute of Medical and Health Sciences, in his article "Psychiatric Stigma: Past, passing and to come," published in the *Journal of the Royal Society of Medicine*, stigma is a mark of disgrace or discredit that sets a person aside from others. It is the process where one condition or aspect of an individual is linked to some pervasive dimension of the target person's identity. It is the negative effect of a label (Hayward and Bright, 1997) or the process of establishing deviant identities (Schlosberg, 1993). Stigma is another term for prejudice based on negative stereotyping (Corrigan and Penn, 1999). Liz Sayce, chief executive of Disability Rights in the United Kingdom and someone very interested in social inclusion and mental health, argues that the focus should move from the receiver of stigma to the people or agency causing the stigma. According to other popular research, she is not the only proponent to call for the profession of psychiatry to change the way it applies negative attribution (Sayce, 2014).

Rejecting the Stigma

Since everyone diagnosed with ADHD has at some time been confronted by its ugly stigma. I feel that it is important to address this burden head-on and empower those with ADHD to redefine the expectations placed on them by society and themselves. Often beginning with childhood, those with ADHD are subjected to disparaging comments about them. Accusations like not paying attention, not taking things seriously, acting rude and disruptive, and worst of all, not caring about themselves and their academic successes is common. When these children get older, they experience the adult version of stigmatizing. They are shunned and accused of *faking* their issues to get out of taking responsibility for their behaviors. Their coworkers avoid them, hoping to avoid being drawn into the problems the worker with ADHD is experiencing. This is not a small problem for those with this brain type. Many live in shame and fear of being found out. Feeling stigmatized causes students to avoid getting the extra help they need. They often feel that their classmates will think they are stupid and incompetent. It causes workers to refrain from disclosing they have ADHD for fear they will lose their jobs. It causes people with ADHD of all ages and from all walks of life to live in constant fear of being ostracized because they are not able to meet the expectations around them. The important takeaway here is that moving beyond stigma can potentially unlock people's potential and how they see themselves and their lives. Rejecting stigma can potentially allow people with ADHD to lead lives with more successful attempts rather than unsuccessful ones.

How can we address this issue of stigma when it is so deeply imbedded in the society we live in? I believe that the way to question the role that stigma plays in the lives of the many people with this brain type is to hear what experts and key people in the field have to say. In this way we would be questioning and hopefully changing the perception where it is rooted. The profession of psychiatry should look at the ramifications of the methods psychiatrists use to apply definitions of disability and disorder because many labeled disabled and disordered may find themselves destined to fulfill what those labels imply. I have worked with people with ADHD who had given up on themselves and their abilities to succeed in their personal or professional lives because of a stigma that makes them feel hopelessly and permanently disadvantaged.

Now let's turn to the history of ADHD and see how the problem of stigma has played out through the years. Through taking a closer look at how psychiatry and neuroscience has evolved in their understanding and description of this brain type, we will discover how the roots of this stigma took hold.

The History of ADHD

Here is a list of the important moments in the history of ADHD:

British Pediatrician Sir George Frederick Still, England's first professor in child medicine, described the first record of ADHD in medicine in 1902. He described forty-three children who had dramatic problems with sustained attention and self-regulation. They were aggressive, defiant, resistant to discipline, and excessively emotional or passionate, and they could not learn from the consequences of their actions. He described their behavior as "a defect of moral consciousness which cannot be accounted for by any fault of environment". He noted that these cases of moral defect without general impairment of intellect is a quite abnormal incapacity for sustained attention (Still 1902)

In 1937, psychiatrist Charles Bradley administered Benzedrine sulfate, an amphetamine, to "problem" children at the Emma Pendleton Bradley Home in Providence, Rhode Island, in an attempt to alleviate headaches; however, Bradley noticed an unexpected effect upon the behavior of the children, namely improved school performance, social interactions, and emotional responses (Bradley and Stroh 2011). However, Bradley's contemporaries largely ignored his findings. Many years later doctors and researchers began to recognize the benefit of what Bradley had discovered (Holland and Higuera 2015).

In 1952, when the American Psychiatric Association (APA) issued the first *Diagnostic and Statistical Manual of Mental Disorders* (DSM), it did not recognize ADHD.

In 1968, when the second DSM was published, "hyperkinetic impulse disorder" (the early term for ADHD) was recognized for the first time.

In 1955, the psychostimulant Ritalin was approved by the FDA and became the go-to treatment for ADHD as the condition became better understood and more frequently diagnosed (Holland and Higuera 2015).

In 1980, the APA published the third edition of the DSM and changed the name of the disorder from hyperkinetic impulse disorder to attention deficit disorder (ADD). It further identified two subgroups—ADD with hyperactivity (ADHD) and ADD without hyperactivity. At this time scientists were determining that hyperactivity was not always a symptom of the disorder. This development tends to coincide with the increase of childhood cases reported or diagnosed at the time. Many speculate that once the disorder was spelled out as ADHD in the DSM-3 in 1968, doctors, parents, teachers, and pharmacy companies got on board in greater numbers. At this time the public at large generally accepted the description of symptoms and treatments for ADHD in children recommended by the profession of psychiatry.

In 1987, the APA issued a revised version of the DSM-3 and changed the name to attention-deficit/hyperactivity disorder (ADHD), wherein the authors combined inattentiveness, hyperactivity, and impulsivity into a single type.

In 2000, with the release of the fourth edition of the DSM, the APA decided to break the condition down again into subtypes, and this time labeled them as follows: combined type, predominately inattentive type, predominately hyperactive–impulsive type.

When one looks back at this history, it becomes apparent that the APA and its members have been searching for the true nature of this brain type for decades and revising its conclusions. One cannot fault the thoughtful research and honest attempts as well as worthy progress made by the profession. But now it is time to take the next step, a step that is overdue. I believe we need to stand back and reflect on where things stand now. How are we serving this population of children, adults, and families? Are we doing them justice by labeling them disordered when the stigma that results from this way of thinking and behaving is demonstrably harmful? Since Freud, the fields of psychology and psychiatry have been evolving, and with predictability, they have been reframing current understandings from one moment to the next, depending upon the thinking and ideology of the time. This is even more of a reason to consider that perhaps it is time for psychiatry to reconsider its thinking in contrast to the growing belief that our job is to understand and accept human diversity, including different learning styles, behaviors, and ways of approaching tasks associated with various brain types. Evidence for this growing belief in the need to support diversity in its' many faces can be found in one of the largest philanthropic foundations in the world, The Bill and Melinda Gates Foundation, which is dedicated to the idea that all people deserve the chance to live healthy and productive lives.

Although the Greeks dabbled in psychology in their day, the profession of modern psychology as a self-conscious field of experimental study began in 1879, when Wilhelm Wundt founded the first laboratory dedicated exclusively to psychological research in Leipzig. Wundt was also the first person to refer to himself as a psychologist and wrote the first textbook on psychology, *Principles of Physiological Psychology* (Wundt, 1902).

There were a number of defining moments in early psychology. One of special importance occurred during the late 1800s when cases of hysteria came to be viewed as a psychological disorder. French neurologist Jean-Martin Charcot utilized hypnosis to treat women thought to be suffering from hysteria. Psychoanalyst Sigmund Freud studied with Charcot. Freud's work with colleague Josef Breuer on the case of Anna O., a young woman experiencing the symptoms of hysteria, helped lead to the development of psychoanalytic therapy.

Most of us are familiar with the early belief that a woman's uterus wandered in her body, causing her to become hysterical at unpredictable times. This meant, according to the experts at the time, that women could not be relied upon or trusted to hold leadership positions and take on responsible roles beyond the domestic duties of home because they may become hysterical when a decision of great importance needed to be made.

Sigmund Freud's work with patients factored heavily in the early days of psychology. His perspective on psychological distress said that it was due to faulty sexual development in childhood. We now know this to be only one factor of all the possibilities that can influence mental health. Freud's theories focused entirely on a person's failure to develop. There was no account taken of the influence of society on one's mental state. In addition, many of Freud's conclusions seemed to justify and pathologize prejudices against those who were traditionally oppressed—women, children, and the sexually abnormal.

Psychological research has also been questionable. In 1939, the "Monster Study" in Davenport, Iowa, experimented on stuttering orphans. Half of the children in the study had their speech fluency praised, and the other half were belittled and told they were stutterers. Members of the latter half were left with a lifetime of negative psychological effects and speech problems as a result of the study.

John Watson, considered the father of behaviorism, used orphans in his experiments. In his study to determine whether fear was an innate or a conditioned response, little Albert, a nine-month-old infant, was conditioned to be distressed at the sight of a white rat. Little Albert was never desensitized to his fear of anything fluffy and white before he left the hospital.

Dr. Henry Harlow conducted experiments on rhesus monkeys and social isolation, placing infant monkeys that had already bonded with their mothers in a vertical stainless steel chamber with no contact for up to a year. Many of the monkeys came out of the chamber psychotic and did not recover. Harlow's students and colleagues criticized his practice of keeping the experiments going long after he needed to, needlessly harming the animals.

These statements are not intended to discredit the field of psychology and those in it. On the contrary, the profession of psychology also brought us important major contributions from the likes of:

B. F. Skinner - operant conditioning theory and the belief that the consequences of behavior determine the probability that the behavior will occur again

Jean Piaget - the theory of cognitive development and best known for his research on children's cognitive development

Carl Rogers - best known for his nondirective approach to treatment or client-centered therapy, where the therapist acts as facilitator

William James - often called the father of American psychology and known for his theories on pragmatism, functionalism, and the James-Lange theory of emotion, which states that our emotions are caused by our interpretations of our own physiological reactions

Erik Erikson - known for his developmental theory and the eight psychosocial stages in which humans develop throughout their life spans, which is in contrast to Freud's theory that personality is shaped by the age of five

Ivan Pavlov - famous for his influence on the development of behaviorism and his theory on conditioning as a form of learning

Kurt Lewin - known for his field theory, which proposed that behavior is the result of how individual traits and the environment interact

The point I want to make here is that psychology, like many professions, is constantly changing and updating itself. At any given point, its theories and practices can only be judged by what is believed to be true at that moment in time. I am thus postulating that based on these facts and present knowledge and experience, psychology will look at the innovator brain type in the near future less like a disorder and more like a different but powerful way of thinking, perceiving, and doing things.

With ADHD, I do not feel in the least that I have a deficit or a disorder. Deficit thinking patterns no longer get in my way or slow me down. I have learned how to make full use of my desirable strengths and to get other people to take care of the rest. I am on the go and on the goal! I believe that one day people will finally get over the negative assessments of rapid-fire thinkers and doers and wake up to the truth. I wonder if one day people will all want to have the so-called ADD brain, and science will be trying to find a way to give it to them.

The purpose of me writing this book was for people to see how difficult it is to grow up in a world that doesn't understand or appreciate you. I want to say, "You can overcome this stigma, and just because people don't get it, that doesn't mean you're not capable of having a happy and fulfilling life." When you let someone's offhanded remark or someone's anger influence how you think about yourself, you are apt to adopt a false identity that will cover up your true identity. If you can't tell the truth about yourself, "I have ADD, and that means that I am more creative and that I need more structure," the message you're giving yourself is, "I'm not good enough to fit in and excel." When you hide yourself, you are also hiding your gifts and the power you have to use those gifts.

I evolved from a frightened, self-loathing child to a place of courage and self-love. With self-love comes freedom, and with freedom comes joy. My hope is that if you have been labeled ADHD, you can end up in this same place of freedom and joy. And if you are not labeled as someone with the ADHD brain type, you will better understand and have compassion for those who are.

ADD is an asset. That belief will be the crux of this book. Working with thousands of people who have ADD and ADHD has taught me that they are infinitely more creative and more adaptable to change than most people who think in a linear fashion.

I hope that this book will open people's eyes so they can see the benefit of viewing the rapid-fire thinking brain type as a valuable asset for everyone and society as a whole. If, as a group, we look at people with the rapid-fire thinking brain type as disabled, then the joy and benefits of their gifts will be lost to us. We always lose when we negate our own worth or the worth of others.

CHAPTER 3

Learning from Four Decades

I began my special-needs teaching career in the 1970s, and I have been one of the forerunners of the ADHD industry ever since. In this chapter I also dig deep into my own journey with ADHD. I cover from my childhood diagnosis of minimal brain dysfunction and go to my current status as a successful business owner.

After four decades of working with this brain type in educational and business settings, I was able to develop a deep understanding of the key elements of brain behavior, strengths, and weaknesses. I remember at the beginning of my career, I was always stunned by the fact that the kids I worked with—those who were being educated in separate classrooms and being made fun of by the kids around them—were actually very bright. When it came to problem solving, they had gifts substantially beyond their peers. They were creative in the extreme and came up with first-class solutions all the time. That's why I kept working with them. I loved the challenge of giving them big problems to solve that were seemingly beyond their years and see them succeed. They had no trouble making exceptional grades when they were challenged and given the opportunity to invent solutions of their own and then apply them to find the best one. They were in my classroom because they were failing in the mainstream classes in middle school.

But it doesn't start in middle school. Kids in elementary school begin getting the message. They can't do what their counterparts can do. They get called out for "acting inappropriate" or shamed because they didn't hear all of the directions. Adults and peers get annoyed. The innovator children try their best to do what is expected of them, but without help to teach them how to do these basic things, they flounder, lose confidence, begin to dislike school, and shut down in certain situations. Wouldn't you also give up if you couldn't do something everyone else could do no matter how hard you tried over and over again to do it? Where is the one person to explain to you what is going on?

This is how it starts and unfortunately continues. This discrimination takes different forms as the child reaches adolescence and then adulthood. After so many years of feeling incapable, not good enough, and anxious, it is no wonder that grown-up innovator brain people can feel angry, suffer problems in relationships, and feel resigned to their fates.

Learning that you have the brain of an innovator helps you go back to your first memory of feeling ashamed and stupid, that initial incident that gets built on over time, that moment when you started feeling bad about yourself. We take you through the process of understanding what really happened back then and what continued throughout your childhood and school experience so that you can look back on your life from your current point of view. Seeing your history through new eyes allows you to appreciate how strong you were and must have been to compensate so well and get to where you are now. Forgiving yourself and others can have a positive and dramatic transformative effect.

Becoming clear on what your strengths, talents, and gifts are is a vital next step to knowing, accepting, and appreciating yourself. When your self-mage is strong and grounded, you can develop the confidence for the work that is necessary to change those unwanted behaviors into new empowered ones, which in turn can lead to well-established habits.

You are now ready to create new self-management strategies so you establish more reliable self-control. Before we get into this step, however, we want you to have the right motivation. The right motivation comes from knowing who you are, what is important to you, and what you believe you can accomplish. We will use the congruency model that will help you become reacquainted with all of your attributes and traits, including those covered up over time by difficult life experiences and lessons. We want you to be able to make good choices and decisions for yourself as a whole and healthy person.

Then it is on to coming up with the best strategies and behaviors that fit your personality and your way of doing things. What are the most important issues you want to address in your life that are keeping you from being happy and feeling like a success story? Choose the top three and get help so that you can establish new ways to address those challenges. Believe that you can do it by remembering that you are a master at compensating. If you have been able to survive this well with less help and incomplete understanding, why couldn't you succeed with good help and a complete understanding?

Developing better habits and ways of doing things will allow you to finally arrive at the destination of this program, creating a new life blueprint for yourself and your future. Having the skills to be the master of your destiny allows you to create a plan for your future and grants you the confidence and resources to follow it through to completion.

My Journey to Find Professional Coaching

When I began coaching adults and adolescents fifteen year ago after a thirty-year career working with ADD in public school environments, I became obsessed with wanting to know why people with the same opportunities, natural talents, and abilities did not always have successful lives. Why did some make it, and what kept the others back? I spent every weekend researching and studying everything I could find about the path of people who became wealthy and accomplished and the path of bright and capable people who did not. I really wanted to know what the difference between those who had lives of accomplishment and satisfaction and those who had lives of struggle and one failure after another was. I began signing up for workshops and training programs and anything I could find that I thought might answer my questions and help me understand how I overcame my own life challenges.

After some time, armed with new insights and more understanding, my search led me to offer seminars and daylong workshops on the subject of "the successful self-image" at local adult education centers and similar venues in and around the Boston area. People said they loved attending my workshops because they were able to put into practice outside of class what I taught them and because they could see the improvement. One day a friend of mine who knew about my endless hours of research and numerous seminars suggested I attend a meeting that this friend had heard about. In the meeting people seemed to be doing what I was doing. This suggestion led me to a meeting where people gathered to talk about their new profession of coaching. Because people had come up to me at the end of my seminars and asked me to work with them one-on-one, I soon discovered at this meeting that what I had been doing with my people seemed very close to the coaching they were talking about. Discovering the profession of coaching was a pivotal moment for me. Almost immediately I loved it as well as the people I met who were also coaching. I soon embraced the opportunity to become formally trained, and I began to develop personal and professional bonds with other coaches.

I shall never forget that pivotal day after a year of doing this work. I sat up in bed and said, "I finally get it. I'm an asset!" That was my true identity, value, and purpose collapsed into one powerful statement that has served me ever since. The idea of *asset* has a powerful synchronicity for me. Powerful synchronicities happen constantly when you bond deeply with your soul's purpose.

My life purpose is to be an asset wherever I go. Within that, my life purpose has to do with saving the natural environment and especially the habitats of threatened and endangered animals. I want to be a beacon to illuminate the path, whether I work with animals, habitats, or rapid-fire thinkers labeled with the word *deficit*.

The way that I related to my family was not working according to my purpose. I came to understand that I was clinging to historical anger, disappointment, and pain from the past, all of which got in the way of me being an asset. I came to see that my rules and beliefs kept me stuck and that I was hiding in my work and making myself busy. I was very motivated at that point to do something about it.

I discovered my ability to forgive and move on. I had no idea how deeply I had been enmeshed in thinking of myself as a victim and how unhappy it had made me until I stopped doing it. I experienced all the happiness in the world when I healed these relationships. When I healed these relationships, I was set free. That's why I believe in the cognitive aspect of coaching. I know that we can change our thinking from negative and self-defeating to positive and self-enhancing. Your life is a mirror of the way you think.

To complete the story of how I wound up where I am today after a career in various aspects of public education, I can tell you that ADD found me. Yes, I had worked with children and adolescents with ADHD in public school environments for many years. Yes, I had relationships with their parents to a certain degree, but my new intention was to coach people to develop a more successful self-image and move beyond the blocks that were keeping them stuck. This could include people with ADD but was not restricted to them. But somehow people with ADD found me, and word got around. Before I knew it, I was having a lot of success coaching them exclusively and really enjoying it.

A Mission in Life

Since then and through the years, I have built a business on my strong desire to help people of all ages with the ADD brain type to overcome the challenges of their misnamed condition. Through the years I have learned how the words *deficit* and *disorder* could not be farther from the truth. My mission became to make it easier for those with ADD to take pride in themselves and their accomplishments so they would end the suffering that had characterized their lives to this point. I wanted them to learn to push back against the lack of understanding and acceptance from the people and institutions around them and become advocates for themselves. If I had been able to learn to overcome my own challenges and struggles, why couldn't they?

My mission became one of making sure that those with this brain type could develop confidence, stamina, and an unflinching ability to believe in themselves. The more I became involved in coaching, the more I realized how coaching was able to do what a diagnosis and medication could not do. It could guide people through a system of behavior changes. Coaching seemed to be the perfect vehicle, and so I threw myself into the profession, getting as much experience and training as I could and as quickly as I could.

Today I have come to the understanding that people with ADHD have unique and inherent qualities, gifts, talents, and the potential to be very successful in what they love to do. This has been my experience over and over again through my work with hundreds of people who live with this brain type. This is what I have assimilated from current and historical ADHD research and what we currently know about the innovator brain. What I have come to understand and believe in is this: When people are labeled disabled and disordered, they tend to act disordered and disabled. If I believe in my heart I have a mental disorder and my brain has deficits, it will become a self-fulfilling prophecy. I will forever look at myself as someone who must settle for being damaged and never expect more.

I now realize that the past fifteen years—and actually looking back on all of my life—has brought me to this moment in time and this juncture in the road. It is time for me to share what I know and what I have learned about ADHD and people throughout these many years. It is time for me to embrace my purpose and help more people with ADHD find their power and use their innumerable strengths to make their contributions and achieve success through the writing of this book. I am excited about the prospect of doing this, and at the same time, I am humbled by such a tall order. Whenever I feel like I am not up to the job, I just stop and think about all the many people who have helped me reach this point in my life's calling, especially the many clients who have taught me some of my most important lessons and inspired me to the greatest degree.

My Core Understandings

It is important to look at the whole human being and how every domain of their life interacts with the others.

We are happy and successful when we live, play, and work out of our passion for what is truly important to us.

Each individual person has a unique energy and spirit that we should strive to know and understand.

Each of us has the ability to be the light that brings people out of the shadows so they can envision a brighter future.

We transform our lives and the lives of others in many small and large positive ways when we are in touch with our life purpose.

We evolve more and more into our magnificent selves as we age and all unfolds exactly as it should.

There is power in love, apology, forgiveness, and gratitude.

We must listen with our heart to the hearts of others if we are going to live, love and work successfully together.

Our greatest gift is the ability to love ourselves so powerfully that we are able to spread that love and kindness to heal the world.

PART 2

Healing Mind, Body, and Spirit

An Integral Approach to Understanding Your Innovator Brain

This section focuses on knowing and managing your innovator brain. Adopting a solid treatment plan provides ADHD innovators with the foundation they need to transform their lives. Highlights of this section include the steps to adopting an all-important meditation practice, instructions on how to create the vital support network you will need throughout your life, the must of a weekly exercise regime, the decision to take or not to take medication for your rapid-firing brain type, and the whys and wherefores of considering alternative therapies.

This section will help you learn how to maximize your gifts and reduce your challenges. It will help you finally makes sense of what has been tormenting you for most of your life. Why do I so easily forget things? Why do I get stuck on doing less important tasks to the neglect of the more important ones? Why is it so hard to be consistent with my routines? Why can't I stop being annoying to others? It is important to realize that the healing of the mind, body, and spirit is a necessary and critical step on the path to adopting a new vision and forward momentum for the future. Healing the past helps to reduce the number of occasions that painful memories will prevent you from thinking optimistically about your potential so that you can lead a more gratifying and satisfying life. Healing the past will help you put your past experiences into the correct perspective when you take on the difficult task of believing you can do what you haven't been able to do before.

Not only will you be shown the steps to renewing your life through a better understanding of what has not been working for you, but you will also find yourself more motivated to try new things because you will have put the right support structures in place to see your goals through to fruition.

CHAPTER 4

Embracing a New Perspective

How would you like to stop living haphazardly and instead start planning to succeed? In this chapter we will be talking about some straightforward strategies that will help you do exactly that. At last you can build confidence in yourself and realize the future you have been longing for.

Three Key Components of a Relaxed and Confident Mind

1. Exercise

Research shows that aerobic exercise actually increases brain mass by growing new capillaries, which is associated with an increase in neural activity. In addition, exercise increases the levels of many brain chemicals, including norepinephrine and serotonin (linked to improved mood, self-esteem, impulse control, and greater focus) and dopamine, which is the major driver of the attention center of the brain as explained by John Ratey, author of *A User's Guide to the Brain*. According to Dr. Ratey, there is nothing that affects brain neuroplasticity as much as exercise. It causes a rapid and persistent uptick in the factors and chemicals that enhance learning and mood. He goes on to say that exercise stresses the brain in a good way, in part by restricting blood flow to the brain. After all, the blood is flowing to your muscles instead of your brain. Just as your muscles deal with the stress of exercise by becoming bigger and stronger, so does your brain, allowing your body to build additional brain matter and synaptic pathways.

In my practice exercise of some sort is key to the well-being of my clients. Because of the positive impact of aerobic activity on the brain, it would be foolish to leave exercise out of the mix. We know its impact on our brain, and it is something everyone is capable of doing in one form or another.

2. Contemplation and Meditation

Many people don't have contemplation/meditation time built into their lives. They don't have the experience of being able to quiet the mind and body amidst the noise and activity around them. As a result, they are missing out on rich opportunities to reflect on their lives and what is most important to them. Meditation can be thought of as the listening part of prayer. Contemplation is similar to sorting through our mental and emotional drawers. People with the innovator brain type feel they can't meditate because it is impossible for them to sit still for the times it takes to get meditation to work for them. To counter this thinking, I regularly send people out into the country and say, "Walk among the trees and leave your technology in the car and don't bring your dog. Walk in nature and see what happens to your mind and to your thoughts." In this way you can connect to your mind and to your true feelings. Writing down what they experienced during their meditations can also help people with this brain type. Writing down one's thoughts afterward helps to reinforce the benefits and usefulness of a sitting or walking meditation practice.

My friend Tom walks a mile in the morning on a circular path in the woods and a mile in the evening. This is his meditation time. Tom is a rapid-fire thinker, and for his mind to focus within, he needs to keep his legs moving. During his walks Tom repeats affirmations like, "I am a caring human being," and spiritual mantras like, "I choose to live my life in deeply satisfying ways." After walking, he sits in a rocking chair and talks into a small digital recorder. This talking takes the place of journaling for him. He goes over his thoughts and feelings and explores the different choices he can make.

Recent research has shown that meditation actually can teach people with the innovator brain how to gain control over their impulsivity. When we sit and meditate with soft eyes and a relaxed body in a peaceful space, the first thing we notice is that our thoughts never stop but keep coming in great waves. As you focus on breathing in and out, you allow your thoughts to come and go. Each time you notice you've drifted, you return to your breath and focus on breathing in and out. By engaging in even five minutes of this practice, you actually learn how to better control your mind. At some point you will find you have greater control over distractions and impulses when you are not mediating. You will have developed more control over what your brain does during normal waking hours.

3. The Mind-Body Connection

We've talked about the groundwork for controlling our thinking. Now let's move on to controlling our bodies. When you find you feel really tired and listless, you have a knot in your stomach, and your body is giving you fear signals, you can do the following:

- Stop. Stop walking, moving, and talking. Be still. Breathe in and out very slowly.
- Put your hands up in front of your face in the halt position as if you are a crossing guard who is telling people to stay put.
- Take a deep breath to fill up your belly and then let it out.
- Do this three times.

- Ask yourself, "What's the most important thing for me to focus on right now?" One possible answer might be, "I need to find out what is going on here so I know how to respond."
- Use the following affirmation: "I'm so happy that I'm learning to control my impulsivity!" The good feeling this affirmation creates in you makes it easier for you to shift your mental and emotional gears.
- Get up and move around. Whenever you're in a depressed or fearful mood, the body sinks into that mood. When you move the body, you automatically get a chance to change to a different state of mind.
- Take a big exercise ball and bounce up and down on top of it for a minute or less. When you stand up, you will feel exhilarated and ready to focus.
- Have a conversation with someone with whom you have a trusting relationship. This is an opportunity to see your value through their eyes. This is one of the most reliable mood changers there is!
- Get something comforting to drink like hot tea and read a favorite quote or passage in a book that causes you to feel hopeful.

You can take the first five bullet points and make them a separate practice. It takes only seconds to do the steps and doing them will quickly give you back your perspective. As you can see by now, when you actively engage in changing the mood you're in, you discontinue the negative feelings that are dragging you down and throwing you off course.

You may want to try hypnosis and various types of neurofeedback, or you may connect best with the very effective tools I have described previously. See what works for you and what you feel attracted to. All of these methods are ways to train the brain to promote a greater sense of peace, patience, strength, and self-confidence. Each individual will experience different degrees of success.

Working with Our Brain

Through the years we have developed a more sophisticated understanding of the interplay between brain chemistry, neurology, and the environment. We now know how environmental factors during formative years contributed to the difficulty we had in managing our rapid-fire brains and how our present-day overstimulating environment has made it even harder to rein in our tendencies to become distracted from our task at hand. In this section we will review the common and specific issues that make daily functioning challenging for people with this brain type and we will offer supportive strategies that innovators need in order to live free of these everyday struggles.

Working with your brain means understanding both the cognitive as well as the emotional side of things. Our past understanding of people with the innovator gene and what they needed told us that diagnosis, medication, and therapy were the answers to a "disabling mental condition". Now we are beginning to understand why that interpretation has not worked for people with this brain type. We are on the verge of finally understanding and seeing this brain type for what it truly is—gifted as well as different. We no longer need any more examples of past and present people who have made great contributions that have rocked our world. We don't need to look at how labeling innovative brain types as disabled and disordered is making them feel and act disabled and how the label becomes a self-fulfilling prophecy. We don't need to look far to understand that doing things in a different way from others does not make one disabled. We just need to let go of the falsehoods—the DSM label and description, the research that continues to promote innovators as disordered, and the narrow-minded thinking that keeps some people insisting that innovators have a brain malfunction. If it wasn't for the brain functioning the way it does, we would be without many if not most of our major scientific, medical, entrepreneurial, and artistic advancements!

For most people with this brain type, I imagine this is very good news and makes a lot of sense. And I know that we are ahead of our time, because it is obvious to me and must be obvious to others that the innovator brain will soon come into its own as the world continues to evolve into a place that has a greater and greater need for innovation to solve growing global problems. As has been true throughout history, we will always need those who are good at innovating and creating the solutions that will save us. It is up to us to teach those with the innovator brain what they will need to succeed, and that process should begin in childhood. In order to do this, we will need to become more educated and better informed.

Deciding to Take Medication

When and if you take ADHD meds depends on the severity of your challenges and how your life will be impacted. When a client says to me, "I think I'm ready to try medication now," I refer him or her to a good psycho-pharmacologist who thoroughly understands ADHD medications. Certain ADHD medications have side effects that are not well tolerated by some people such as loss of appetite, loss of libido and a racing or buzzing feeling in the body, among others. Some people philosophically disagree with putting such chemicals in their bodies. Yet for others it is like a light just got turned on, helping them to stay focused and on task. For each individual, success with medication can take time, and changes to the dosage and the type of medication may be required to get it right. I encourage people not to get discouraged. The end result may well be worth it.

Once people have their first prescriptions, I help them monitor how it's working, and I make sure they stay in communication with their doctors.

CHAPTER 5

Knowing Your Own Mind

People with this brain type make up for their impulsivity and lack of focus by using their innate talents of curiosity, creativity, high energy, and problem solving. It is important here to remember that impulsivity can be managed with good habits, but the natural creativity of ADHD cannot be taught. In this chapter you will discover how understanding your mind and how to use it to the greatest advantage allows you to experience more happiness, success, and fulfillment.

The following five cognitive strengths of your innovator brain will always be your superpowers.

Cognitive Strength 1: Compensating

The ability to compensate in an environment of different personalities and ways of thinking is one of the great cognitive strengths of this brain type. Compensating in this case basically means making up for what one is not good at by using what one is good at. Another way of saying this is that these people can use their inherent strengths to manage their weaknesses. This ability to compensate gets developed early on in life as a way to make up for difficulty with paying attention, being impulsive, lack of planning ahead, poor task and time management, and in general, many of the functions human beings engage in when they can motivate themselves. Typical compensating mechanisms that people with this brain type commonly use include the following:

- creating a successful outcome to a project through last-minute effort,
- using sharp intellect to make up for lack of attention and preparation,
- assimilating all components of a subject quickly and coming to a conclusion, and
- knowing how and where to efficiently find answers to perplexing questions.

Often people with the innovator brain come to rely too heavily on their abilities to compensate. This eventually gets them into trouble when their abilities to compensate begins to grow thin as they get older and more is expected of them. Typically the compensation ability becomes inadequate at some point in middle school, high school, or college. Sometimes the problem is put off until these people experience trouble adjusting to the demands of their first jobs. But when it does happen, it always catches people by surprise, and it can send them into a tailspin from which they cannot recover without help. People with the innovator brain type need to understand how this works so they will recognize it when it happens to them, will know how to address it, and will not let it completely throw them off. I have heard many clients tell me they were okay in their lives until something big happened to overwhelm them, knocking them off balance and preventing them from believing they could continue to compete. They tell me that's the point at which they begin to think they never had a competitive advantage in the first place.

Compensating is a stroke of genius and a helpful mechanism, but like all strengths, it cannot be counted on to carry the whole load.

Cognitive Strength 2: Routine

Recurring routines are the best friends of the innovator. Once a routine has been established and repeated often enough that it is a habit, the innovator can continue to use it to comply with the expectations and demands around them.

Innovators are natural rebels and mavericks, not always agreeing to go along with a demand. While this may appear to be a bad thing, more often than not the innovator has a better idea and a good reason to want to use it. The companies that listen to them are often happy they did when it results in an important improvement or a solution to a vexing problem.

People with the innovator brain need help establishing their routines, and they also need people to hold them accountable so that they maintain those routines. They can learn the process of establishing routines and practice applying it with the helpful oversight of a coach or mentor. Once they learn how to keep their routines going, they can expand their repertoires to include other domains of their lives, such as keeping a schedule and keeping up with errands, projects, and relationships outside of the workplace.

It is also important for innovators to get help when a routine changes in any way. Otherwise they run the risk of returning to their old ways when the new way doesn't seem to be working anymore. It can be devastating to fall back into an older problematic routine after you have worked so hard to succeed at your new and better one.

Cognitive Strength 3: Creativity

One of the great cognitive strengths of the innovator brain type is the extraordinary ability to come up with creative applications and solutions to many head-scratching problems. Because the brain thinks so rapidly—a quality of the rapid-fire gene—it can filter through many possibilities in seconds and come to a conclusion quickly. This is important because creativity can give humans a competitive advantage culturally, entrepreneurially, economically, scientifically, and artistically. When you are capable of thinking creatively and efficiently on your feet, you are able to offer immediate solutions based the best options available at that moment in time. This can be especially helpful in emergency and time-limited situations. Many very intelligent people who do not have the asset gene will also be advanced creative thinkers. Although innovators are not the only ones blessed with this trait, they tend to excel at it more than linear-thinking brain types.

Additionally, innovative gene holders don't give up. Unless they are told to stop, they can keep improving on their ideas ad infinitum, and that is why deadlines are sometimes necessary to hold them in check. Left to their own devices, innovators like to keep going and continue to improve and make things better. *Sufficient* and *good enough* are not concepts that come easy for them. They will need to learn to structure their tasks into time frames and do what they can within those boundaries—unless, of course, they are trying to find a cure for cancer.

Cognitive Strength 4: Problem Solving

People with the innovator gene love challenges. In fact, challenge is a requirement if they want to avoid getting bored and seeking stimulation elsewhere. In particular, they love the challenge of how to solve serious problems and dilemmas that hold back people from making important advancements in industry, commerce, medicine, and government. Innovators also learn best when they are learning in the context of a challenge, finding a better answer, solution, improvement, or direction to go in. They do best when they learn in context so that they can see the purpose to their works and how they all fit together.

Like creativity, problem solving is a similar gift of the innovator gene. Innovators have a quicker turnaround time than the population at large. Their answers are often high quality and well suited to solve the problem. Because innovators thrive on discovering the hidden solutions to issues, having an innovator around can be a great asset. And because this ability is so highly valued, you often find them in the fields of technology, science, law, finance, sales, and management. After all, how may hundreds of experiments did Edison perform before he was able to invent the light bulb? How many theories did Einstein investigate before he came up with his famous game-changing one on relativity? How many years of studying, painting, and trial and error did Picasso log before he came up with cubism, and how many years of failure did Lincoln have before he reached the presidency? It is either known or likely that all of these people had the innovator brain type and none of them gave up on themselves and what they believed in.

Because the innovator brain often seeks the challenge of solving problems, this also gets translated into taking risks. Many people with this brain type are race car drivers, astronauts, skydivers, and stuntmen. Their brains thrive on taking risks that will produce the adrenaline they crave because of a lack of dopamine. Taking risks can also assume the form of playing games of stimulation. "How late can I leave and still make it to work on time?" "When do I need to make the deposit so it's there just in time for the checks to clear?" "How much other stuff can I do and still get my work completed before I go home?" Unfortunately these are not always good games to play, and they can get in the way of being productive, meeting goals, and completing tasks. Alternative ways of seeking stimulation will need to be explored and mastered so that these stimulation-seeking games do not get in the way of accomplishments and leading a balanced life.

Cognitive Strength 5: Collaboration

What is collaboration? Is it the ability to work with someone in order to get something done? Is it the ability to get along with someone else's opinions, ideas, and decisions? Is it a desire to fulfill a goal in order to benefit someone or something? It is all of these elements and more because it infers that the intention of the collaboration will be shared by those involved.

Not all collaborations work out the way they were intended. For innovators to be good at collaborations, they will need to (1) agree on the intention of the collaboration and (2) agree to the ground rules for working together. Additionally, the success of the collaboration will ultimately depend on (3) how motivated the collaborators are to succeed and what they have to gain or lose.

Collaboration also depends on each member of the team recognizing the strengths and gifts of the others. Without this recognition, the team will not assume its best functionality. This can be an ideal landscape for someone with the innovator brain to shine. Identifying where they can offer the most value will allow innovators to use their talents to the best of their abilities. This way they can avoid wasting time and energy on the things they don't do well and will inevitably get stuck on. The project or collaboration will need to be broken down into steps with reminders, resources, and deadlines in place so the innovator can comply with what is expected of them. Depending upon the parameters of the collaboration, it is a great asset to have regular check-ins with someone involved in the collaboration so that straying from priorities does not become an issue. As we move beyond an insistence that innovators are disordered and into a framework of what we can teach them about organization and self-management and begin to realize what we can learn from them about creative ideas and solutions, we will find that all of us can indeed work together productively.

CHAPTER 6

Informing Yourself about Medication

The decision to take or not take medication can come from our own personal research, advice from trusted professionals, a medication trial to ascertain the effects on our body, and an understanding formed over time of what is best for us. To shed further light on the subject, we will examine the results of some case studies and talk more about how medications actually work in the body.

A Five-Year-Old Boy on Ritalin

Before I started coaching, I worked in public schools. I was just out of graduate school, and I was helping a new director start a special education program in Georgia. We were working with kids who had diagnoses ranging from nearly autistic to more minor behavioral issues. One child in particular was a little five-year-old boy who could not sit down to save his soul.

He was just beginning the first grade, and he was often not where he was supposed to be or doing what he was supposed to be doing, a common story for children with the innovator brain. He was constantly bumping into people and knocking things over. This caused continuous interruptions for his teacher and classmates who had to wait for him. They often lost patience with him. He knew he was supposed to be still and follow directions, but he couldn't control his behavior. He got in trouble constantly and his self-esteem was really taking a beating. We called his parents in and told them that we were going to have to try something new to help him and his teacher. This happened in 1973. At that time in our history, we still weren't sure what we were doing with medications for children. But with this child, we had already tried several behavior plans and interventions, all to no avail. Although this was a new experience and something I hadn't handled before, I felt at the time that the only thing we hadn't tried was medication.

Initially the director of the program backed away from suggesting a trial of medication for the boy, thinking the child was just too young. But I kept pushing for it. Finally the day came when the director was willing to meet with me and with a psychiatrist who was on board with the idea. We agreed to propose to the parents that we try the medication route, promising to carefully monitor the program every step of the way. After several conversations the parents finally agreed. I think they were equally exhausted with his behavior at home. At the time the approach to medicating children was much more conservative than it is today. So we were prepared for parent and professional pushback when word got out. It never came. The results of giving this little boy Ritalin were quick and nothing short of miraculous. He was able to sit down in his seat for short periods of time and pay attention. He could control his movements better and stand in line without bothering other kids. Although his attention span was still shorter than his classmates', he was not getting into trouble as much. He was feeling better about himself, and he was demonstrating the ability to learn in school. We did carefully monitor him. For the three years I knew about this child, it was amazing to witness his positive growth. No one at that time was giving medications to five-year-old children. But I couldn't help but feel that this child was being saved.

As the years passed, I have seen over and over how ADHD medications can be an effective agent for improving the ability of the brain to focus. I've also seen them not work at all. On occasion I saw how they could have a detrimental effect on young children when they were not monitored carefully. A child's growth over time will signal when there is a need for a change in medication. And once a child gets older, the obvious hyperactive behaviors begin to diminish and take on a different form, sometimes described as "type-A personality characteristics."

Adults who take medication have more or less the same experience as children and adolescents. Medication helps people of all ages with the innovator brain to calm down, act less impulsively, focus, and concentrate. It's very difficult to learn and absorb information when you can't pay attention. While children need medication to be successful in school, adults need medication to be successful at their jobs and get those projects done at home so that they keep their promises to their partners. Medication works differently on every single person. Certain medications are effective with some but not with others, not to mention the possible manifestation of certain side effects. Medications for ADHD now on the market tend to be safer than other medications because they do not build up in the body. So while that is good news, the downside of these medications is that you may need to try a number of them until you find the one that works best for you. In addition, some people don't like the way medication makes them feel, and others are philosophically opposed to putting chemicals into their bodies. For all of these reasons, it is important to see a doctor that specializes in medications prescribed for attention deficit disorder so that you can start out on the right foot and get the right kind of care.

Dale's Story

Dale was in his late forties. He was getting ready for his boss to fire him from his fourth job. He couldn't tolerate being sacked from job after job anymore. He came to me because his wife suggested he try something else, and after he put it off for months, Dale finally followed his wife's suggestion and called.

Dale and I began meeting together, and by our third appointment, it came out that he had been refusing to take medication as a way to help him with his inability to stay on task and deliver his projects on time. He had grown up with parents who had taught him that putting any kind of chemical into his body was wrong and would ultimately harm him in some way. In the coming weeks, Dale and I talked a lot about what was now known about ADHD meds, including the upside and the downside of taking them. He decided that he wanted to learn about these medications and know the truth so he could make up his own mind.

Dale decided to try a prescribed ADHD drug under the care of a well-informed doctor that was experienced with ADHD medications. At first Dale said that taking the medication made him feel strange and that he wanted to quit. We both wondered how much his reaction was psychological and how much was physical in nature. So we made an agreement. If he would stay on it faithfully for the duration of time the doctor recommended, he could quit if he chose.

At the end of the trial period, Dale and I took an accounting of his experience with the new drug. Dale reported that he had gotten used to the way it made him feel and wasn't uncomfortable with that any longer. He reported that the uncomfortable feeling had gone away. He also reported that his focus was better and that he was able to stay on task for longer periods of time. While he still wasn't able to get his projects in on time, he was not getting so far behind in his work, and he felt if he kept working on it, he could meet his deadlines better.

Dale reported that he had never been able to stay on track with his tasks before, and even though his wife was still not convinced Dale's changes could be relied upon, she did admit he had been taking time to communicate with her—and really listen to her—something he had not done in in years.

The last report I received from Dale said that he had not gotten fired from his job. Instead he had been put on a performance improvement plan. Because of our work together, Dale had learned enough from coaching that he was able to teach his boss what he needed in order to manage himself effectively on the job. His boss was being cooperative. He evidently valued Dale's contributions enough to do what was needed to help Dale succeed.

What ADHD Medications Actually Do

In order to consider the innovator brain as an asset and not a deficit, one must look at the practices in use today to manage the daily challenges of someone living in the noninnovator linear world. These challenges among others include getting started on projects, keeping up with them, and completing them within a time frame. Since the innovator brain can best be described as the inability to inhibit behavior, anything that requires an organized focus for a prescribed period of time (e.g., a project) is difficult to complete. As soon as the novelty wears off and the lack of interest sets in, it becomes necessary to create a chain of stimulation. We're getting bored. So our attention now shifts. We look for something interesting, and like following a shiny penny, we detour from our course, fully intending to return to finish the project. Sometimes this takes the form of diving into more interesting aspects of our project, which eats up time and throws us off course.

The problem is that often we don't finish or we don't finish in time. This is not because we cannot do so but because we have not been taught how to manage the difficult task of maintaining focus.

One thing leads to another ... and then another and then another, and being people who live in the here and now, we can lose track of big swaths of time and get ourselves into trouble. When people with innovator brain types have been given free rein to work in ways that best suits them, even though it may not fit with prescribed practices, they are capable of creating masterworks of invention, science, medicine, art, and technology. Doesn't it make sense to give them the structure and help they need to complete projects and expectations in a way that works for innovator brain folks and noninnovator brain folks alike?

With this idea as a lens through which to view the innovator brain, we can now discuss medication as a way to address the situation previously outlined and others like it. Let's consider medication as one way to help people with innovator brains *fit in* and *make their contributions* more easily. I have seen ADHD medications make a huge difference in people's lives, and in many cases it has saved the self-esteem, education, careers, and marriages of many innovative individuals who felt doomed.

So what do ADHD medications do? A basic explanation says that chemical reactions cause the fire of dopamine/norepinephrine into the prefrontal cortex of the brain and thereby stimulate the person. Without dopamine/norepinephrine, the brain gets bored, so it goes looking for something to give it another kick. That something may include such behaviors as moving around, talking, playing video games, surfing the Internet, or any number of other sensory experiences. Amphetamine drugs like Ritalin stimulate the brain enough so that it does not have to create its own stimulation. In short, meds keep the brain awake and involved.

All of the executive functions, such as starting, stopping, paying attention, holding multiple ideas in the brain, and responding to questions, happen slowly or not at all when dopamine is missing. On the outside this can look like the person without enough dopamine/norepinephrine has a low IQ, is lazy, or doesn't care. But this is not true. Though those of us with the innovator brain struggle to respond appropriately to the demands of our environment, we are far from stupid. In a sense, we need to remember we are more like stimulation-seeking missiles. We need a higher rate of revolutions per minute to get us going, so we move faster and more often. We're looking for the shiny penny, that stimulation that will *wake* our brain up.

Kids with rapid-fire thinking wait until the night before to study for a test because the adrenaline takes the place of what's not happening in the brain. The brain reasons, "At least I've got adrenaline." The problem is that people with the innovator brain are smart enough to produce top-notch papers and projects at the last minute, so they think that their winning formula is staying up all night. But that's not true. Their true winning formula is finding a way to stimulate the brain so they can tap into their reservoirs more steadily over time without waiting for the adrenaline. Then the real brilliance will have time to express itself more fully.

When ADHD medications create dopamine/norepinephrine in the brain, this allows the synapses to fire so that behavior can be inhibited. A beneficial medication allows the innovator to move their attentions from one thing to another with thoughtful control. When you have control, you can learn structures, develop routines to support you, and build a network of helping people around you. You will always have a need to inhibit certain behaviors, but eventually you learn to create the stimulation you need within safe boundaries. With the help of a coach or other professional as well as medication, you have taught your brain to master better habits realizing reliable routines and measures for self-control. Off medication, you may again experience the same historical difficulty of inhibiting certain behaviors like impulsivity, but you will have the benefit of new habits that will allow you to stay within safe boundaries.

Older Adults and Medication

Adults in their fifties may have been put on Ritalin as children. When they were young, that may have been the only choice available to them. Unfortunately in the 60s and 70s, doctors and parents didn't know what we know today about taking Ritalin. People back then did not completely understand the possible side effects and how the drug would affect their bodies. Patients would suddenly not feel like themselves, and the professionals around them would have no explanation to help them understand what was going on inside their bodies. They would have difficulty eating and sleeping, and then they would come crashing down. They couldn't pay attention, and their crashes could happen anytime, even possibly in the middle of a test in school. One central problem during the initial uses of Ritalin was that people didn't understand when to take the drug. They would take it at the wrong time and not when they most needed its effects.

All adults will most likely benefit from being brought up to speed on what we now know and can do with these medications. I typically share with my clients basic knowledge and information that I have learned from my own training and experience. I tell them about the medications we have now and basically how they work. I help the parents who want to understand the reasons to medicate or not medicate their children, the high school or college students who are having trouble getting their academic works done, and the adults who are struggling to live up to expectations at work and/or at home. With a better understanding, they learn how to talk to their doctors in an educated way. Fortunately today there are many drug companies coming out with different combinations and choices that allow more and more people to find medications that work for them.

Sometimes people who have had a bad experience with pharmaceuticals or drugs may not want to talk about medications. They don't want to have anything to do with them. Younger people who are brought up in families where prescription drugs have been abused sometimes refuse to consider medication. There is also a subculture of people who believe that any additives or medications are bad. Whether or not they have an understanding of how these medications actually work, they have an emotional reaction to the idea of trying medications that will depend on their experiences and beliefs.

I help my clients understand the physiological changes that take place inside their bodies when they take ADHD drugs so they can have confidence they know what they are doing, especially since these drugs are considered by many to be some of the safest on the market. I also like to share with them what some recent studies and experts have to say about the place of medication in the treatment of the symptoms of ADHD:

- "The drugs usually prescribed to treat attention-deficit/ hyperactivity disorder (ADHD) are generally effective and safe. Most children and teenagers, about 60 to 80 percent, who take them become less hyperactive and impulsive, are better able to focus, and are less disruptive at home and school" (Consumers Union 2012)
- "The risks of using these medication are very low," says William W. Dodson, a Denver-based psychiatrist who specializes in ADHD. "The risks involved in not treating ADHD are very high. These include academic failure, social problems, car accidents, and drug addiction." (Dodson 2015)
- In the largest study ever of ADHD treatments, researchers funded by the National Institute of Mental Health found in 1999 that the most effective treatment was a combination of behavioral therapy and ADHD medications. (National Institute of Mental Health 1999)
- In March 2005, researchers from the University of Buffalo SUNY found that behavioral modification therapy allowed doctors to significantly lower the doses of ADHD

medications that children need to take. (University at Buffalo, SUNY, 2005)

It is a well-known fact that ADHD medications do not build up in the body like antidepressants (SSRIs) and other drugs prescribed for mental health issues. That is why it is easier and takes less time to measure the effect of different types of ADHD medications at different doses when one is looking for the best match. That is also why it is easier to stop taking these medications without worrying about having to manage potentially difficult withdrawal symptoms.

Long Term Negative Effects

Longitudinal studies have so far not proven there are adverse long-term effects from taking ADHD medications.

An example of a popular study is that of Dr. Rachel Klein, PhD, professor of psychiatry at the New York University School of Medicine, She did a two-year controlled study of more than 100 school aged kids back in the late 1970s and then followed up with them repeatedly over 33 years. Most are now 41 years old and those who took ADHD medication showed no negative effects in terms of medical health or other functioning, compared to those who didn't" (Klein, et al 2012)

An example of two studies conducted by The Wake Forest Baptist Medical Center and John Hopkins based on research with animals found that the long term therapeutic use of drugs to treat ADHD does not seem to cause long term negative effects on the developing brains of children. The John Hopkins Study done at the same time as the Wake Forest Study using older animals and different drugs had similar findings (Pierre et al, 2012)

Clearly there needs to be more research in this area as conflicting evidence continues to surface on the possibility of long term effects. The good news is that adverse reactions usually happen within the first few weeks of taking the medication, allowing people to stop or switch the prescriptions early on.

Best Two-Step Practice for Taking ADD/ADHD Meds

If you are ready to consider how medication could make life easier and more rewarding for yourself or a family member, then you could consider the following steps:

The first step is to find a psychopharmacologist type of doctor who understands how to prescribe these meds. A regular doctor often has to learn while you're learning, but someone who specializes in ADHD meds rather than your primary care physician is already light years ahead and can save you time, frustration, and money. Finding an ADHD psychopharmacologist may be a problem for someone in a rural area, but with the help of the Internet and a willingness to travel a longer distance on occasion, you can do it. And it's important.

The second step to take is to gear up for a trial-and-error process. You may need to try three or four meds before you find the one or the combination that works for you. If you have a professional who's experienced, then you can cut down on the mistakes and get to the right dosage sooner.

It is important that people understand that there is no one fix for low dopamine/norepinephrine. However, some combination of medication, coaching, therapy, and other practices like those previously outlined can be helpful and in some cases transformative. It is possible to learn strategies to manage behavior and gain self-control to a greater extent as a result of taking medication in combination with coaching or therapy. Most importantly, you can't allow yourself to get discouraged. Keep trying. You're creating your future. You can do it with support. Through this process of working together with someone who is there to hold you up and hold you accountable, you can discover your ability to create a really good life. You *can* make new habits with daily routines, systems, and structures that will allow you to be successful with your relationships and your work.

CHAPTER 7

Exploring Alternative Healing

Termed comorbidity, many diagnosed with ADHD have secondary conditions, such as depression, anxiety disorder, obsessive-compulsive disorder, bipolar disorder, and post-traumatic stress disorder, just to name the most common documented ailments. These individuals in particular can reap great benefits from alternative therapies like neurolinguistic programming and eye movement desensitization and reprocessing. The following alternative therapies have proven to be the most helpful alternatives for my clients. Not all alternative therapies can be included here, so I have chosen my favorite ones at the time of writing this book. I encourage my readers to try new things, to have open minds about the new developments all around us, and to trust their intuitions, another asset of the innovator brain. These techniques will either be helpful with your anxiety and trauma or useful on a regular basis to manage behavior and emotions.

Neurolinguistic Programming (NLP)

The basic premise of NLP is that the words we use reflect our inner subconscious perception of our problems. If these words and perceptions are inaccurate, as long as we continue to use them and think of them, the underlying problem will persist. Our attitudes are a self-fulfilling prophecy (www.holisticonline.com/hol_neurolinguistic.htm).

In their book *Neuro-linguistic Psychotherapy,* D. Bridoux and M. Weaver say, "NLP does not have the same model of 'problem' and 'solution' as clinical psychiatry, instead its model is based upon helping clients to overcome their own self-perceived, or subjective, problems rather than those that others may feel they have."

The approach does not focus on the past but instead focuses on the present and future. The NLP counselor uses curiosity to invite clients to envision their preferred futures, and then counselor and clients start looking for the perceptions and interpretations that are getting in the way of that future. The counselor asks questions about the clients' stories to see what language might add to the problem's persistence. By looking for exceptions to the problem, the counselor and clients can potentially change the language to describe the problem and in effect change the problem, providing a solution.

You can actually use this approach yourself by going through a NLP training program or learning from a trained practitioner.

Emotional Freedom Techniques (EFT): Pattern Interrupt

If you have a pattern of behavior that is keeping you stuck in negative thinking patterns, you can use a pattern interrupt technique such as the one Kay Snow–Davis suggests in *Point of Power: A Relationship with Your Soul.* She says,

Place the finger tips of both hands in the center of your forehead and move them apart toward your temples several times, stroking lightly to release emotions and stress. After you erase the physical and emotional tension, command that your random thoughts STOP: then focus on moving your mental energy to your heart. (You can command your mind to 'Stop and Drop!' to drop this energy downward to the heart.) Take a deep breath; then continue to focus on your breathing as you experience the power and stillness of your heart energy. In this way your mind can hear and receive truth and guidance from your heart.

At those times when you find yourself lost in discontent and unease, notice your mental chatter, and use the erasing motion of your hands on your forehead as a pattern interruption. Remind yourself to "stop and drop." This will help you become more aware of your own innate power when your heart and your mind are in partnership and balance.

This is merely one technique of many to get you started in this wonderful practice. There are a number programs and trained people out there where you can find out more.

The Power Breath

Kala H. Kos, author of *The 7 Lost Secrets of Ecstasy and Success: How to Awaken Your Hidden Power for Love and Riches*, talks about the power breath. She says,

To experience more of your innate power in each moment, it is also helpful to turn your attention to your body and your inner energy field. To do this, let me introduce you to a technique I call the Power Breath. It will charge you energetically and relax you into the present moment. Simply begin by noticing your breathing. Now, as you inhale, put your attention on the crown of your head, and as you exhale, put your attention on your navel. If you find it useful, place one hand at the top of your head and the other at your navel as you begin. Keep shifting the focus of you attention from crown to navel with each inhale and exhale. Since energy flows where attention goes, the mere focus of attention on these two areas will begin the flow of energy between them. Release your hands at any point you wish, and continue the Power Breath for at least 8 rounds. You can practice this technique anytime, anywhere, with your eyes open or closed.

I use the power breath technique. I have found it to be an effective and quick way to access my own truth and wisdom in the moment.

Eye Movement Desensitization and Reprocessing (EMDR)

EDMR is a comprehensive, integrative psychotherapy approach. EMDR psychotherapy is an information-processing therapy. During this therapy the patient relives the stresses that have helped create anxious patterns. Memories are brought up, and then the therapist helps clients change their thought patterns by changing their bilateral eye movements and introducing tones and taps. The client basically reprocesses and eliminates triggers by focusing on a set of external stimuli that override those triggers. There's a lot more to it, and EMDR does not work for everyone. However, it does work amazingly well for some people. It is worth your time to investigate it if you suffer from anxiety that prevents you from dealing with conflict in a neutral and open manner.

Ho'oponopono

This is an ancient Hawaiian healing system and so much more. Using specific exercises and teaching new understandings, this system helps you clear out your past negative experiences and memories so you can get to *zero* and embrace your present opportunities. Getting to zero means not having to struggle with what has been holding you back from success and happiness. The premise of this system says that your past holds memories that block you from being free to pursue your true potential in every moment and that unless you work to take full responsibility for everything in your life, you will continue to find obstacles in your way. It is one of my most trusted practices, and I highly recommend that everyone check it out. Consider checking out the following: *The Easiest Way* by Mabel Katz, *Zero Limits* by Joe Vitale, *Getting to Zero* by Joe Vitale, and the website http://www.hooponopono.org.

CHAPTER 8

Reinterpreting your Past

A lack of self-confidence is almost always a result of growing up with an innovator brain type. As I have done with hundreds of clients, I provide the basis for rebuilding a sense of self-respect. This process includes meditation, power statements, and progressive visualization exercises. This is about healing the old story and reinterpreting the past by removing self-blame and self-condemnation. Many people have tough histories with this brain type. Therefore, we need to give attention to rewriting the script. It is very important to address whatever shame the client feels so that it can be replaced with understanding. I have found it to be of the utmost importance that people learn to trust themselves if they are going to move forward into a better future.

I'm convinced that a lot of people who have made genius contributions are people who are different and who have the rapid-fire brain type. Although our country has historically been considered a melting pot of people coming together successfully from all parts of the globe, we've also been a prejudicial, exclusionary melting pot. As we have seen throughout our history, elitist and exclusionary conformism hasn't worked. Whether we're negatively judging people on the basis of their cultures, their religions, their races, their different socioeconomic standings, or their ADD/ADHD, we can be a prejudiced bunch.

Almost every person knows an individual who is a rapid-fire thinker. We don't always recognize them, but as we learn to educate ourselves about their different ways of thinking and approaching things, we will learn that rapid-fire thinkers are part of the bigger picture and that they make a contribution to us all. As we move away from labeling an innovator brain as a disorder, a dysfunction, and a brain malady, everything is going to change. Right now, looking at the innovator brain as dysfunctional keeps many of us stuck in old ways of thinking. We continue to ask ourselves how gifted contributions to the world can possibly come from such dysfunctional minds. Nevertheless, it takes a long time for human beings to let go of superstitions and negative perceptions.

Rapid-fire thinkers are the consummate entrepreneurs. We need entrepreneurs. We need innovators. Entrepreneurs are being asked to step up and save the American economy. Entrepreneurs need more than the ability to creatively solve problems ten times faster than other people. They also need the support of others who believe in them and who can help them create structure for their ideas.

That's why this book is for rapid-fire thinkers and for the people who appreciate them. For the world to receive the gifts of the innovator brain, there will always be the need for individuals who are not rapid-fire thinkers to stand back and take a look at how an idea can be brought to the forefront. We need the people who say, "Wait a minute. Hold it! Great idea, but here are the factors that we need to handle to get your solution to work." Overseeing and reviewing are actions that describe what our partners, friends, and bosses must take for us to realize the benefits of our contributions. And that's great because rapid-fire thinkers are at their best when they are up against challenges. Let's listen to Sarah's story.

Sarah

Sarah was a thirty-four-year-old married mother who had always felt that no one approved of her. A long time ago, Sarah had learned she was inadequate, and therefore, she felt that she would have to work much harder than anyone she knew just to eke out an existence. She could never hope to be good at anything or happy like she perceived the people around her were. They weren't stupid. Sarah was. Her energy needed to be directed at minimizing her stupidity and mitigating potential disasters of her own making.

One of Sarah's earliest memories of great sadness happened when she was five years old. She had just started kindergarten, and it was time to come in from the playground. Sarah was doing her best to pay attention to what her teacher was saying, but there were so many distractions. Everything seemed to be happening at once. So when everyone was told to sit at their places with their special animal pictures and the teacher got to Sarah, she couldn't remember what animal she was. She froze and stood there. The teacher asked again, and Sarah looked in horror as her teacher shook her head and reminded Sarah that she was in kindergarten now. If she wanted to stay in kindergarten, the teacher told her, she needed to start listening. The teacher then pointed out Sarah's seat. Sarah remembered how exposed and inadequate she felt in that moment. In that moment she knew that she was not as smart as the other children. It was then that Sarah's confidence and her excitement that she was in kindergarten began to fade. She wanted to run away and hide forever. As similar incidents of not paying attention and forgetfulness continued to happen, Sarah's bad opinion of herself was reinforced. School would not be a safe place for her.

Flash forward to when I met Sarah, and you will find she has built her life around the idea that she is inadequate and dumb. Sarah has the innovator brain, and she has shown herself to be highly gifted academically in college. She was a first-rate team leader and problem solver as a project manager. Yet Sarah continues to sabotage her accomplishments because of her very low opinion of herself, which started all those years ago in kindergarten. Such is the fragility of a small five-year-old child and the power of an erroneous belief that gets reinforced over time. Sarah was never stupid or incompetent. Sarah had a different type of brain that didn't fit in with the majority. Sarah has talent and skill beyond measurement, and for the first time in her life, she is beginning to see that could be true.

Sarah is learning how to rewire her brain by impressing upon her mind new ways of seeing herself as competent and gifted. Through coaching, Sarah is learning how to reinterpret her past through a different lens. Instead of seeing herself as the flawed child, Sarah can view herself as the misunderstood child because of the inability of others to help her understand herself. Sarah sees the importance of this work to heal her heart and mind as necessary if she wants to be the whole valued person and mother to her girls she wants to be. Because Sarah has agreed to focus on her accomplishments and attributes instead of her ill-perceived flaws and inadequacies, she has begun to catch herself when she self-sabotages and to stop the behavior. Sarah's roles as parent, wife, and a career woman are all looking up and will continue to improve as long as she is willing to stay the course of healing her life and becoming the woman she was always meant to be before that five-year-old little girl fell off track.

Negative Labels

I have a new client named Claudia, a young newlywed whose parents are upset that she told her professor she has ADD. They are worried she will be labeled and treated differently to her detriment. Her husband was the only person in her life (until I came along) who encouraged her to share her ADD way of thinking and doing things. Claudia realized that she trusted her own abilities more than her parents trusted her, even though she acknowledged that her parents only had her best interest at heart.

Acknowledging one's thinking type out loud to society doesn't have to be taboo. The idea of labeling does not have to mean that the rapid-fire thinking type is a bad thing. ADD/ADHD does not have to be a stigma. Would labeling your child as an accomplished musician be a bad thing? Would labeling yourself as bright, creative, and inventive be a bad thing? I don't know, but I have noticed that people tend to go for what they consider to be the positive labels and avoid what they consider to be the negative ones. What if ADD/ADHD was a label to be proud of like other positive labels?

It's up to us to make that so. We can insist that the brains of rapid-fire thinkers are more akin to a style and way of thinking especially pronounced in creative and inventive ways. But as a society, we've developed the habit of perceiving ADHD as a negative. Eventually innovator brain types will get better at advocating for what we need, and I see it happening right now all around me. The world is full of capable people not living up to their potentials. Many of them have self-esteem issues and anxiety or depression, and some of them have more serious mental problems. But I think there is a solution brewing out there. My observation is that the further along we get at understanding, accepting, and appreciating one another's differences, the more we'll be able to accept ourselves as good enough and worthy. It all comes down to loving and accepting ourselves as a foundation for loving and accepting others.

The decision to self-identify is a personal one. We have to work out for ourselves and our children what would be in our or their best interests. Since this sort of disclosure can be tricky territory to navigate, it helps to involve a coach or therapist in the conversation and decision-making process.

If you are a rapid-fire thinker, you can think of yourself as a super-evolver. Super evolved people are able to see the solutions to future problems before others are able to see them. Without the perspective of your brain as an asset, you will live in a world that you feel negates who you are. You are very likely to continue your current practice of struggling to get by. But if you take hold of the true strengths of your innovator brain, you can overcome your weaknesses and triumph. With help, you can be the one to push through the naysayers and opt for using your strengths to manage your weaknesses. And with support, like everyone else, you can learn to be more self-accepting of the mistakes you make as a necessary part of making progress.

It seems we get the notion early in life that we need to change ourselves in order to fit in with the expectations of the world around us. As we perceive how people respond to us, we sometimes get the impression that we're not doing the right thing and we're not as smart or as competent as others. Because as children we do not yet have the ability to reject negative assessments of ourselves that others may make, especially if those people are older than we are, we tend to believe what they say. We believe that our parents, teachers, other adults, or the popular kids at school know better than we do. As we grow, such negative looks, comments, or actions toward us get logged into a negative file in our minds and add to a growing list of the bad things we need to change about ourselves.

The fear of being shamed, looking foolish or stupid, or appearing less capable than all the others is a powerful motivator to not trust ourselves. We begin to learn we cannot safely be the people we naturally are. We must always be on guard. As fragile and vulnerable children, we can begin to see negative meaning everywhere we look, and so we begin to look for it everywhere. Fear of ridicule can be a potent killer of healthy self-esteem. When our spirit is continually in the line of fire, it gets wounded and eventually learns to hide out and fade into the background.

Talking about this issue of self-doubt is critical to understanding how to work with your brain. We must know how self-condemnation works to help us avoid it. Reinterpreting the past pain and struggle through understanding it is a necessary component of healing and moving forward in our lives. Our spirit wants to be free of feeling unacceptable. Soul deep healing involves asking the following question: How could we have done things any differently if we didn't understand why we were not able to do what the people around us did so confidently? Soul deep healing means we let go of the belief that we are incompetent. We must take on a new understanding of our true assets and admit that we have not gotten the help we needed up to this point.

Self-Acceptance

When you struggle with unacceptable behavior and difficult emotions, you lose confidence in yourself and have problems communicating. You struggle and suffer on your own because you are down on yourself. Let's discuss how you can gain control over your impulsive tendencies and unfocused behavior. It's time to let go of anxiety and live in the joy of being you.

From Suffering to Succeeding

My family moved around a lot when I was in my teens. I remember arriving at my eighth high school and feeling immediately out of place. Everyone there wore designer clothes, and they had the kind of money I did not have. I felt like an outcast in a group of kids with expensive homes and nice stuff. That was my assessment of the situation. Those were the thoughts that created my reality.

I thought if I took a public-speaking class with the popular kids in the school, I could get to know them, and then maybe I would feel like less of an outcast. Signing up for the class did not change that. Nor did it help me feel included and accepted. Instead it backfired on me.

In the class we had to write and deliver a speech about what we wanted for our future. It was my turn, and I quickly realized I was too nervous to stand up in front of these kids and give my speech from memory. I would have to read it. But that was not the worst thing that happened. In the speech I mentioned things that I thought the popular kids would approve of like how I would drive a Jaguar, play several instruments, and have a lot of money. I named the top boutiques where I would shop. When I finally looked up, all of them, including the teacher, were looking down. I didn't know what to do, and I began mispronouncing words. In spite of the snickering, I completed the speech before I sat down.

The teacher then stood up and said, "This is an example of a poor speech. First of all, it's not honest. Secondly exaggerating did not impress us. And your speech was poorly executed because you read it and couldn't pronounce many of the words." I felt humiliated in front of a group of high-achieving peers.

Today I can look back at myself in that situation and see it differently. Because of many geographical moves and family issues, I realize now that I had no confidence in myself at that time in my life. I identified with being worthless and flawed and feeling marginalized. I understand now why I did not just stop speaking and say, "This isn't going very well, and I need to rewrite my speech". I knew after the first few minutes that I was in for a humiliating experience. But back then I was struggling to understand the rules that everyone else lived by. I literally did not know how to behave. The volatile problems I had to face within my own family had left me in such a vulnerable position that I did not possess a well-formed identity in my teens.

Self-Identity Thieves

Like me, you may have been telling yourself a lie all these years. Lies start by saying or thinking, "I'm not good enough. What's wrong with me?" It helps to understand why some parents hurt their children. They do it primarily because they see the children as objects. Whether it's just during a time of stress or it's a lifelong continuation of the way they see themselves, parents can objectify their children. When people see others as objects rather than as human beings, they are in a sense abandoning those individuals. They are not really listening or paying attention to their unique feelings and needs.

Typical negative feedback that children, especially rapid-fire thinking children, hear include the following:

- "What's wrong with you?"
- "Why can't you measure up?"
- "How many times do you have to be shown something before you can do it?"
- "You never listen to me."
- "You don't care."
- "You must be doing this on purpose."
- "We're going to have to refer you to a professional. We've tried everything, and nothing works."

Hearing these messages over and over again will drive the perception of low self-worth deep into a child's consciousness.

Do any of them ring a bell with you? Do you remember hearing such things when you were growing up?

Affirmations and Taking a Stand for Yourself

Here are some powerful affirmations you can try on. Later in this book, we will help you write affirmations of your own.

- "Like everyone else, I have strengths I can rely on and limitations I can improve on."
- "I am an asset."
- "It makes me happy and proud to become more empowered and true to myself."

- "I feel good about my unique qualities and how I am getting better and better every day."
- "I know deep down inside I am capable and competent."

In time, if you keep saying that last affirmations, your affirmation will become this: "I am capable and competent," which is a more powerful stance. And if you keep saying that, you can't help but become capable and competent because your brain and body will direct you to think and feel differently. The good feeling will spread, and you will start behaving differently and more in line with being capable and competent. That's how it works.

Proclaiming Our Assets

As we've talked about, an important aspect of soul deep healing is developing healthy self-esteem and confidence in ourselves and being acknowledged and recognized for our talents and strengths. Those of us who are grown adults may need to go back and heal our past childhood and adolescence if we did not receive this acknowledgment. As parents, adults, and teachers, we need to remember the importance of doing this for the benefit of the children in our lives now. We need only remember back to the time when we were growing up and needed someone to say the following:

- "Who can run faster than you?"
- "Who can put toe shoes on and do a solo performance as beautifully as you?"
- "Who is so good with animals?"
- "Who can make cakes that are as good as yours?"
- "Who else is so good at telling/writing stories?"
- "Who is better at math than you are?"
- "Who can be a better friend than you?"

Steps You Can Take

Sometimes believing in yourself is just the hardest mountain you've ever had to climb. Here are some intermediary affirmations when you just can't swallow the idea that you are wonderful, worthy, loving, and competent. Intermediary affirmations start with the phrase "I am learning to—"

- "I'm learning how to put my money away," is an intermediary to the statement, "I have lots of money."
- "I'm gaining control of my procrastination," is an intermediary to the statement, "I have no problem with procrastination."
- "I am so happy now that I am learning to think before I act as well as appreciate my strengths and talents."
- "I love that I am working toward a place where I feel comfortable taking risks to get ahead and becoming permanently better organized."
- "I'm proud of how I can think positively about being successful and loveable."

What you believe about yourself is what matters. Affirmations work best if you believe them, but they will work if you keep saying them whether you believe in them or not.

Sometimes my clients listen to me talk about affirmations and say, "It can't be that easy." It either is or it isn't, depending on your belief system. Saying something is easy. Believing it can be easy or hard, depending on how clearly you can see your own thoughts influencing you. The ego wears many disguises to keep us from seeing that we are responsible for creating our own pain as well as our own pleasure. The ego wants you to believe that it was the man who assaulted you, the mother who didn't love you, the brother who bullied you, or the sister who made fun of you that caused your life to turn out the way it is now. The ego wants you to believe that you are a victim. This sort of thinking can become a habit that leads to great delusions and even deeper sadness. As we discussed in chapter 7, affirmations, meditation, and contemplation are powerful tools for taking back the open mind and believing heart you had as a child before you began blaming yourself.

Your Deciding Factor

I believe that the tipping point between solid, grounded life success and shaky failure is how you feel about yourself. Self-esteem is the core issue of ADHD, and adopting good self-esteem determines whether you will experience more confidence and success in your life or more self-doubt and failure.

We all get into messes. Without being conscious of it, we create pain and self-sabotage. This applies to everyone in the world. But the difference between success and failure is the difference between saying, "I'm a loser," and stating, "I'm strong enough to overcome this and keep going."

When we look at the world with an open mind and heart, it is easier to believe we're here on this earth to learn compassion and love. That's it. It's not so much about material possessions, having a lot of money, or being better than others in our lives or our careers. We complicate life when we make it about anything except learning how to love and care for ourselves and others.

When a rapid-fire thinker can discover a truer course for his or her life without feeling the victim of a disorder, he or she gains clarity. When you know what you're looking for, you can find it. So when you face scary circumstances, it's good to have tools that help you assess the situation. For instance, if your boss is mad at you for doing a poor job on something and you're afraid you're going to be fired, it's better to keep your head and your confidence to turn the situation around. Don't allow yourself to spiral downward and direct anger inward.

If you're not satisfied with your life, there's still good news. The ability you used to create your present situation is the same one you can use to change it. Only you can reverse the direction of your life.

You have the power to change your circumstances. The first step to successful change is vision. Create a vision in your imagination. Write it down and revisit it at least once a day. Believe in yourself. A vision is seeing yourself performing on stage and convincing others with the confidence of a successful speaker. For rapid-fire thinkers, creating visions is fairly easy. We can create ten visions a minute. The tricky part is being able to stay with one vision and believe that we can and will see it manifest.

Being married to a vision is being comfortable with being uncomfortable. If you want to change things, you will need to learn to live with some discomfort and fear. Marrying your vision is accepting that it's going to feel awful sometimes. The people around us may get upset with our changes and even try to interfere. This makes us even more uncomfortable. Here is a common scenario. You work hard to improve your performance on the job. You stop fooling around and adopt a vision so that you can become a master at what you do. If you're a rapid-fire thinker, you're likely to surpass your coworkers and maybe even your boss. Suddenly your friends at work are telling you they're worried about you and can't understand your behavior. Your boss starts making it harder for you to succeed and leaves you out of the communication loop. When we begin to experience greater success, we will need to learn to steel ourselves against naysaying and jealousy. It comes with the territory. Our job is to get comfortable being uncomfortable and keep going anyway.

Two Perfect Tools

How can you endure discomfort and self-doubt without giving up? Two very helpful strategies I have found to work for many of my clients include (1) creating and saying empowering affirmations and (2) making a habit of the spiritual practice of meditation. I should preface this by saying that for rapid-fire thinkers, being still may mean bringing calmness to their minds while their bodies are moving.

Contemplative Meditation: Connecting to your Inner Voice

As we talked about in chapter 4, meditation is the opportunity to let go of stress and negative thinking and listen to the true voice deep inside of our being. Contemplation is sorting through our mental and emotional drawers. But we don't have to sit for hours in the lotus position in a quiet, distraction-free room with a fountain of running water to have a successful meditation practice. I regularly send people out into the country and say, "Walk among the trees and leave your technology in the car and don't bring your dog. Walk in nature and see what happens to your mind and to your thoughts." Connect to your mind and to your true feelings. Either then or when you return to home or your car, write down what you discovered on your walk so you can capture these precious moments.

Remember, by building an understanding relationship between yourself and your brain, you affirm your worth and achieve greater self-acceptance and self-confidence. Being quiet and still through a meditation practice that works for you helps get you there.

PART 3

Healthy and Happy Relationships

I believe that satisfying relationships are key to life success and fulfillment. That is why it is so tragic that those labeled ADHD suffer so much in this arena. The reason for this can seem like a complicated mix of bad behavior and self-centeredness. I agree that ADHD behavior can certainly look like that! But the reasons for relationship problems being at the heart of ADHD dysfunction are more easily understood when we examine the history of those labeled with it. As children, we learn to anticipate failure as the pattern of response we can look forward to in our environment. Eventually we begin to try anything to avoid it, including lying and shutting down emotionally. Imagine the frustration of continuing to make the same mistakes over and over again and having neither insight nor help in addressing them! That's the legacy of growing up with ADHD.

In part 3, we will dedicate chapters 9, 10, 11, and 12 to enhancing personal relationships in the workplace and at home for people labeled ADHD. As innovator brain types, we typically have communication issues with wives or husbands and bosses or managers in particular. But we also have communication breakdowns with friends, coworkers, parents and/or children. The good news is that we can learn to value ourselves enough to learn from these communication breakdowns and improve our relationships.

CHAPTER 9

Innovator Brain Communication

Those of us who suffer under the ADHD label would agree that poor habits of communication negatively influence our relationships. Oftentimes we do not respond to others in a timely manner or we may forget something we were asked to do and end up making excuses and apologizing. We may feel so bad about ourselves that we avoid responding altogether. These repeating patterns of miscommunication can look to others like we don't care about the task - or them - and serious consequences can result. To make matters worse, over time we develop a mindset of self blame and give up on our ability to meet the expectations of the important people in our lives.

The truth is we don't need to give up on ourselves and our relationships. We can do much better.

Understanding Is Key

How we understand others and how they understand us is key to having a fulfilling and joyful life. To the degree there is misunderstanding and inadequate or misguided communication, our relationships suffer, and we can feel isolated and alienated in our lives as a result. This is truly the heart of suffering in all of us. Ultimately this is the cause of many mental health problems.

Good communication first depends upon how positive we feel about ourselves. Most of our problems with communication result from our own negative emotions, and those can lead to misunderstandings with others. It is vital to understand the real source of any issues we are having with understanding and being understood by others. We must learn a proactive way to express ourselves without allowing negative assumptions and unwanted impulses to get in the way.

I remember years ago when I was sitting down at a meeting and planning an event with a group of people. We were hard at work trying to make some important decisions. Suddenly the person who had the floor stopped midsentence and began yelling at me for constantly interrupting the group. The degree of anger she expressed shocked me. I felt attacked, and I also felt like a failure as a person. Did I realize I was constantly interrupting them? No. Neither did I realize anyone was upset. I felt like I was crumbling inside, and I kept my mouth shut for the rest of the meeting. I couldn't wait to get out of there.

The next day after I had recovered from my wounds, I asked myself how I thought I had cocreated that outburst. What had I done to cause something I was completely unaware was going on? Then I started to pay attention to the times I interrupted others and learned these instances were considerable, but most people were too timid to make me aware of them. I began to pay attention, counting inside my head before I spoke as a way to restrain my impulse to say something when someone else was speaking. I kept a pad of paper beside me at all times so I could write down what I wanted to say and not forget. I took the experience and used it to become a better group participant. I worked with a coach to gain control over my impulsivity.

A cousin I'm close to never writes thank-you notes or calls to say that packages I sent with gifts in them have arrived on her doorstep. For a while I kept quiet and decided that she just didn't care. After I learned more about how to negotiate and resolve conflict, I was able to say to her, "Please let me know the gifts have arrived and what you thought of them. I don't want to be left with the feeling that you don't care."

In this case, I expressed my feelings to my cousin instead of having a conversation with myself. I stepped out of fear into self-love and truth. Before that, I was just making up the whole thing in my head without knowing the truth of how she really felt.

When you love yourself, you're willing to take a stand for yourself and create your experience instead of resigning yourself to the same old negative interpretations that leave you feeling alone and empty. You can decide to focus on the positive and uplifting result you truly want to have as your ultimate outcome. You become willing to get help so that you can maintain truly caring and generous relationships. It all comes back to appreciating and accepting ourselves for the unique difference we make in the world.

The Source of Conflicts

With rapid-fire thinkers and innovator brain types, impulses can come from a strong desire to help out or gain approval, but can look like violating boundaries or dominating or disrupting others.

In addition to filtering through our impulses before we act, we also have to decide how we are going to deal with conflict. So many of us lived with trauma and conflict all the time while we were growing up. We made the decision at that time that conflict was painful and needed to be avoided. Unfortunately that just isn't true. We must learn to move away from being anxious and avoiding conflict. We have to learn to use conflict so that we can have self-fulfilling outcomes as we seek to create whole and happy lives.

Sandra's Story

Sandra walked into her friend's house for the first time on a social visit. After she asked to excuse herself to go to the bathroom, she wandered around, opening closet and cabinet doors to look inside. She was just curious, but by snooping around, she had violated her friend's boundaries. Her impulse to see everything dominated her desire to respect her friend.

Her friend caught her in the act when she started wondering what was taking her so long. Sandra was embarrassed and fumbled around for an excuse, saying she was looking for a clean towel. Sandra's friend stopped calling, and when Sandra and I met, she told me that her primary reason for seeking me out was to get help with her issues. She was continuing to lose her friends, and she was angering her sisters and coworkers because of her overly curious behavior, which they usually referred to as snooping.

Rapid-fire thinkers with the innovator brain type can appear strong and in control, but deep down they may harbor a feeling of low self-worth. Every day they can come into conflict with others, and the message they take away says, "I'm incapable of measuring up." Sadly low self-esteem is the very reason why so many of us need to seek professional help and why it is vital that we employ new ways of thinking. It is also the very reason we don't seek help. We just don't want to fail again or acknowledge our failures in front of another person.

It might help you to realize that conflict is not a bad thing. Even if conflict scares you, you have to admit that without conflict you would not even be alive. Without the conflict between stasis and movement, we would not breathe. Without the conflict between stasis and hunger, we would not eat. Without the conflict that our parents went through to find each other and to create and support us, we would not have come into the world.

As a rapid-fire thinker, you can learn to put conflict to good use. When you harness conflict with the intention of creating good outcomes, you naturally form mutually beneficial relationships. Let's talk about how that is done.

Successfully Handling Conflict with Others

We are going to be looking at how to create more harmony and agreement in relationships by addressing communication issues head on. We will find out how three women learned some important lessons in how to address conflicts in particular situations. The following case studies were chosen because it is likely you will find the stories familiar or even similar to your own.

Brenda's Story

I have a client named Brenda with an anxiety disorder. Brenda has a fear that people don't like her. She worries she'll be rejected because she always makes a fool of herself. Brenda avoids having real conversations with anyone because she's afraid of saying the wrong thing.

Her sister's boyfriend said to her one day, "I think you're spending too much time over here." She stoically packed her bag and left. She never came back, and she never talked with her sister and her boyfriend about how to establish more comfortable boundaries within which they could all live.

Through our work together, Brenda is learning how to communicate more honestly with her new roommates in her new living situation. She began her new relationship with her roommates by telling them about the difficulty she has expressing herself and advocating for what she needs. Her roommates appeared understanding at first, but it has been hard going at times. All behavior change takes time, and it is up and down. As of this writing, Brenda is spending more time out of her room and not ready to give up. Through coaching, she has learned to appreciate her small steps.

In American and Western societies, we are discouraged from expressing anything that goes against the program laid out by our parents, schools, etc. We stuff our feelings and don't know how to handle those feelings and thoughts that do not go along with the group's way of doing things.

When you believe that conflict is not safe and not permitted, you will be filled with conflict. When you say to yourself, "I will not have this conversation. I will not express what needs to be said. I will not ask for what I need," you give anxiety, fear, and alienation a way inside you.

I remember sitting in a meeting of church members in someone's home in the early 70s. It was a palatial home, and most of the people were at least a decade older than I was. I was in my early twenties. The topic of conversation was drug use and how to deal with the hard-core drugs and substance abuse of the young. Finally after I sat quietly for a long time and listened to drug users being stereotyped as those who shot up or smoked illegal drugs, I cleared my throat and added, "Drug use isn't confined to the young or to illegal drugs. Many people abuse prescription painkillers, sleeping pills, and antidepressants." I then added, "There's also alcohol." The room grew quiet.

Finally one woman said, "Yes, that's true." I felt good about myself for speaking up, and I will never forget how hard it was to go against the program in that room.

Because of their natural inclinations to push back, rebel, and argue, those with innovator brains have an even stronger "no conflict" program hanging over their heads. In other words, society comes down even harder on those who rock the boat. Rapid-fire thinkers get in trouble a lot by breaking rules and acing like mavericks. Rapid-fire thinkers don't learn the lesson like the other kids. At first they may not stuff their feelings down, but soon they will learn to.

Most innovators eventually will get the message, "I don't fit in, and being different is difficult and painful."

People labeled ADHD can have a low awareness of how they are coming across. They need people to give them feedback in caring ways. In the workplace they need others to take the time and make the effort to tell them how their gifts and talents are important to the organization. They need to be reminded that like you and everyone else, life and circumstances will always ask us to grow and improve. Sometimes people are afraid to give feedback and are afraid of confrontation. Whether or not a rapid-fire thinker is open to receiving feedback depends on the caring part. If you say, "The way you handled that is completely wrong," they may not listen. If you do care about their input, a better way to talk to them is to say, "I value your contribution and don't want you to keep making the same mistake. My suggestions are intended to keep us working together effectively." It's important that the rapid-fire thinker remains open to hearing the feedback and is willing to work collaboratively to make changes.

Cheryl's Story

Cheryl is a creative person in her industry where she works in the upper echelons of a marketing firm. Although she's worth millions to her company, she consistently upsets colleagues and clients, unaware that she comes across as uncaring and insensitive. It took her a while to realize why people did not seem to like her, and it took some persistent people in her life who cared enough about her to get her to listen to them.

Initially the marketing firm Cheryl worked for hired me in a last-ditch effort to keep her. They had come to the end of their ropes, and even though they stood to lose initially by letting her go, they wanted to move on. Our work together couldn't bring changes quickly enough to save Cheryl's job. She was let go, and soon she quit coming to our coaching sessions altogether. Eventually I heard she found another job and got married.

After about a year of marriage, her husband asked her to start seeing me again. She agreed, and we began to work on a wide range of issues. When we began meeting again, Cheryl confided to me that she hated her new job and that it was way below her skill level. She was taking antidepressants and knew that she was drinking more than she should. Our first job was to work on Cheryl's state of mind and her feelings of discouragement. Then we could move on to bringing her back up to speed. In the process Cheryl learned how to listen to feedback from someone else, her ADHD coach in this case. As Cheryl learned to actively listen, she found that her coach was in complete alignment with her. It was then she learned that if she trusted the process and her coach and if she agreed to try out new insights into her own behavior, she could learn a more successful way to communicate.

It has been three years since Cheryl came back to coaching. One day at a time, she puts another bead on the string of self-control, self-awareness, and self-love. These were the keys to Cheryl developing the ability to communicate effectively, specifically her ability to care enough about how she talked to and treated other people. Cheryl had not had good role models for effective and caring communication when she was growing up. But Cheryl's amazing progress shows that it is never too late to learn a vital skill.

Her evolved ability to creatively solve problems coupled with her new life skills and caring ways of speaking with and enlisting the help of others makes her an invaluable person. Cheryl is a prime example of how it is possible to enjoy all the benefits of being a rapid-fire thinker by smoothing out the rough edges that go along with it. It took time and effort for sure. But for the rest of Cheryl's life, she gets to reap the benefits of being a whole person. She is able to bring her innovator brain skills to make another company a leader in the digital marketing industry.

A Common Communication Killer

Do you sometimes blurt something out, argue, and forget to pay attention? When most people encounter rapid-fire thinkers who interrupt others or mistakenly blurt out something offensive, they will walk away or just ignore them. Especially in today's world, people won't necessarily take the time to understand another person's behavior. Getting to know a charming, intelligent person and then discovering there is another side to this person when he or she starts acting like an uncontrolled teenager is disconcerting and confusing.

Here are some helpful suggestions you can memorize so that they become part of your thinking and available when you need them. It is terribly difficult for people with innovator brains to not blurt and say what they're thinking, offensive or not, when their brains lack the basic ability to inhibit such behavior. But armed with previously prepared responses to use or remember, it can become easier for them. These can be reminders of our need to develop more self-awareness in our interactions with others, especially those with the innovator brain type. Consider the following examples for the innovator: "I've noticed that sometimes when I talk, I talk over you. I know it makes it hard to carry on a conversation with me. It's okay to stop me when I do that, and I will try not to interrupt." You could also say, "Excuse me. Could we wait a minute? I got distracted, and I missed what you just said. Can we move over here where it is less distracting?"

Now consider the following examples for the other person: "I respect you and think you would want to hear this. Sometimes you blurt out things that people can take the wrong way. Understanding you like I do, I know you do not want to be misinterpreted." The other person could also say, "You seem to be feeling frustrated and overwhelmed right now. How can I help you with that?"

Harmony in Relationships

The more harmony in a relationship, the more easily conflict can be openly discussed. Showing someone your anger is a sign of trust and a desire for continued intimacy.

My own inability to express conflict stemmed from the fact that there was so much conflict around me when I was growing up. I felt like there wasn't room for any more, so I kept to myself and did my best to avoid getting involved. In my family we had to stifle the conflict because there was no way to express it without all-out chaos. I learned to be very uncomfortable with arguing.

Some of us are predisposed to anxiety and depression either as a result of trauma or because we inherited this tendency from our parents. Some rapid-fire thinkers have anxiety disorders or suffer from depression, and it makes them fearful or panicky when they are confronted with the possibility of conflict. But disagreements and arguments are a vital part of communication. They help us to clear up confusion with the people who are important to us so that our relationships flourish. Therefore, sooner or later we all need to come to terms with this important communication tool, namely coming to agreements.

Strategy for Creating Agreements

One strategy to participate in a talk you would rather avoid is to begin the conversation when you are both doing something fun and cooperative together like driving in the car on your way to a vacation, cooking dinner, taking a walk, or planting a garden. In that way conflicting emotions are less likely to get triggered. Both of you will begin the conversation at an emotionally neutral point. Then at the right time you can bring up the topic you have been avoiding.

Many rapid-fire thinkers find themselves isolated, but they can't figure out why. They are unable to see themselves as others do, and few people can or will help them do that. Like any relationship, sticking with an innovator means creating an understanding between the two of you. Remember, someone who has been diagnosed with ADHD spends his or her life trying to adapt to what other people consider normal behavior. These individuals must work hard to fit into a prescribed way of being. Even with all this effort, they will not be able to avoid making the same mistakes while their self-esteem takes hit after hit. Oftentimes they won't see these hits coming. They don't intentionally mess up, and often they aren't sure what they've done wrong. Innovators have to focus so intensely and courageously to get through the day that they often do not have the energy to focus on the needs of others. It is all they can do just to meet the expectations around them and do their best to manage their behaviors.

As we have said, the two areas of life most critical to happiness and good mental and emotional health are undoubtedly the areas of communication and relationships. How we successfully or unsuccessfully communicate with key people in our lives determines the outcome of our relationships both personally and professionally. If you question this assertion, take a look at your life now and in the past. Find one painful experience that did not originate as a result of a bad relationship or the parting of a good relationship. Often we don't understand the impact this has on our lives. We wonder why we are unhappy and tend to blame it on outside influences like a bad economy, a bad job, a bad break, or fate. In our choice of justifications, we forget that at the heart of each of these explanations is an issue we're having with at least one of our relationships, even if the relationship is the one we have with ourselves. Relationships and how we communicate with others determines the confidence we have in ourselves, how empowered we feel in our lives, and the degree to which we are able to love and trust. This helps us explain why difficulty with relationships is reported to be the number-one problem being addressed in therapy and coaching.

People with the innovator brain suffer the most from having felt and continuing to feel misunderstood and unaccepted. They come to fear communicating because they are so used to getting it wrong. Because of ongoing criticism from others, they develop a strong belief that they are incapable of communicating successfully. They shut down and give up or learn to depend on others to do things for them. It's usually a combination of both reactions. When we say nothing or don't give enough information so that others can understand us, we actually end up creating the situation we are trying to avoid. Our tendency to play it safe actually has the opposite effect.

Emma's Story

Emma was a bright, hopeful twenty-five-year-old who had recently graduated with an advanced degree and just landed her first professional job in telecommunication. But for all her intelligence, creativity, and exemplary skills, she had never taken control of her poor communication habits. Emma had never been in a work environment without the structure and support of teachers, professionals, counselors, and parents.

Early on Emma had developed a fear of speaking out because it seemed that whenever she did, she invariably said something stupid or wrong. She was also prone to interrupting and blurting things out without thinking. Since childhood, she had learned how to avoid these tricky communication issues by working around them. She would use e-mails, notes, high grades, and the helpful intervention of others on her behalf. Emma's inability to ask for help and take responsibility for her own communication had so far not produced serious consequences. Because of these compensating mechanisms, Emma was not motivated to work on this issue or change her behavior.

Emma learned quickly at her new job that things functioned differently in the workplace. Coworkers, supervisors, and staff members around her were taking care of their own professional responsibilities. There was no one who looked remotely interested in helping her. Emma found herself in a situation for the first time in her life where she had no one to go to for help. She found it extremely hard to get her work done because she had so many questions that needed answers first. Emma became despondent and took to hanging out in her cubicle and avoiding coming into contact with anyone. She soon fell very far behind in her work and began taking sick days off. Emma had begun to seriously question her ability to hold down a job and succeed in her career. To sooth herself and to block out any thoughts about her situation, she began to use marijuana and drink alcohol at night. She soon came to the point where she had almost entirely disengaged from her job. When she was asked to meet with her supervisor, she just didn't go. Emma stopped showing up at work and never answered the phone when human resources called to inquire into her whereabouts and her plans.

Not long after, family and friends began to notice something was wrong with Emma, and they were finally able to convince her to spill the beans about what had happened with her job. Under her parents' guidance, she moved home, stopped drinking and smoking, and started taking antidepressants. Her family and friends could not believe how down and out Emma had become. They discussed their observation that she seemed to have completely lost faith in herself. Emma was put in contact with a therapist who agreed to work her as long as she met with an ADHD coach on her issues with communication. Emma said yes to these suggestions, and she and I began our work together with the help and support of family, friends, and professionals.

At first Emma and I worked on understanding the causes of her failure to be successful at her first job. She needed to get beyond blaming herself and all the people who let her get by without developing the tools she needed for employment. Once Emma began understanding how this had happened to her and why, she was able to forgive herself and others. This in turn opened the door to investigating solutions to her communication avoidance patterns. The challenging part for Emma was practicing her new communication strategies. Putting herself in the position of possibly looking foolish tended to bring up old painful memories. We started with small steps and simple communications with people she knew well. From there she started to explain things to complete strangers, and finally she started to ask for help and advice from authority figures and people who were important to her success in the workplace.

As of this writing, Emma is searching for a new job with renewed confidence in her ability to communicate and overcome issues that arise. She feels that even though she knows she has a way to go, she has learned to trust herself and her ability to overcome obstacles by asking questions and building helpful relationships. She is learning that she doesn't need to be perfect in everything she does and that it's expected that she will make mistakes and learn from them like everyone else does. She has discovered that she is more competent than she gives herself credit for and that believing in herself will get her through the rough spots. We are working together less now, but we still check in with each other on occasion. When we do check in, Emma shares with me how she is getting help from the right people and is feeling more connected to and accepted by those around her. She hadn't realized how hard she had always worked to be acceptable in the eyes of others until she stopped doing it, and she felt that a large burden had been lifted from her shoulders.

Many of us suffer from a fear of being humiliated or shamed in our relationships with others. But the price we pay for shutting down is worse. It takes courage to express ourselves and accept that it may not always go the way we hope. The good news is that we can learn to understand ourselves and our faulty communication patterns. We can control them, improve them, and come out on top. Like many worthwhile things, it takes practice, commitment, and a good support system. But since effective and rewarding communication is one of the most important skills we will ever have, it seems worth the time, effort, and whatever price we must pay.

You can assess how you are doing in the area of communication within your personal and professional relationships by determining the following:

- How often are you asked to explain what you're talking about?
- How often do people get frustrated because you do not appear to be listening?
- How frequently must people contact you because you have not responded within a reasonable period of time?
- Are you giving people the impression that they can't rely on you to do what you say you will do?
- What are the real consequences in your life because you are avoiding important conversations?

Of course, if you answered yes to any of these questions, it may be a good idea to seek help. Observe the degree of dysfunction that any poor communication habits are causing you. Admit to yourself that it's worth a try to learn something new and change some behaviors that get you into trouble. Ask yourself what would be possible for your life if you did get better at communicating. Don't continue to let a lack of successful communication spoil your relationships and opportunities.

CHAPTER 10

Finding Yourself through Your Work

The tips in this chapter can be put into use immediately, mitigating common stumbling blocks for innovator brains like missing deadlines and not having a structured and systematized work environment to support task completion.

Disclosing You Have ADHD at Work

Remember Claudia? When Claudia realized that she trusted herself more than her parents trusted her on this particular issue, she set up a meeting with her boss and spilled the beans about what she at that time she called "her condition." It turned out that her boss knew there was something going on that could explain how such a bright and capable person could be so unreliable.

It ended up being a great relief to both Claudia and her boss, who even agreed to pay for her to work with me. Claudia was amazed at how being completely honest with someone about her challenges with "always making mistakes," the thing she most feared people would find out about her, had paid off in such a positive way. Claudia reports that this experience has forever changed her feelings about herself and other people. Seeing herself as capable has allowed her to stand up for herself and get the help she needs to work with efficiency, effectiveness, and confidence in her place of employment. She and her boss have built a more trusting relationship with each other, even though her boss says she can still be frustrating to work with at times. As always, it comes down to self confidence and self esteem.

The Importance of Innovators in the Work Place

I do think that we humans are slowly evolving and coming around to living our true purpose on this planet. As we are advancing mentally and spiritually, not everything will be advancing with us. Transformation can be messy. But I believe that we're all here to get better at being human, to help others, and to save our planet for future generations. In her book, *Intuitive Management,* Joia Jitahidi uses the phrase, "Our work is our work" (Jitahidi 2004). I love this quote because I believe she is saying that the occupation or career we have is going to present us with the mental, emotional, and spiritual challenges we need to work on in this life. I think people are finding that our spiritual nature matters more than we ever thought. We are beginning to realize that when we are at our best, we are tapping into the wisdom of that spiritual side of us.

These days a popular slogan in the business world is, "Human capital is our most valuable asset." I happen to believe it is true that the people who make up a company really are its backbone, far more than even the products or services it offers. After all, those change according to the market. While I believe that this is true, I also have seen strong evidence over time that the managers of many companies do not act in accordance with this view. While they may throw around popular slogans about valuing their people, they are not offering the leadership to back it up.

For more than thirty years, I have seen valuable employees with the innovator brain type misunderstood and disregarded like rejected cogs in a wheel. Unfortunately many businesses operators see their employees as interchangeable parts and are more willing to spend ten times the money to replace them than spend a small amount of time and money supporting them in positive, expansive ways.

Clearly innovative thinkers with their higher than average abilities to solve problems would make ideal employees during a time of global expansion. What we find instead, however, are many rapid-fire thinkers stuck in uninspiring jobs, struggling to stay employed in order to make a living.

Sadly managers don't know how to manage someone who comes across as disorganized and unpredictable, who is lacking in accountability and late for work, who is slow getting their assignments in, and who forgets to communicate. They don't know how to respond to the impulsivity and distractibility of these workers. But here is the rub. These same employees have contributed solutions, ideas, and new processes that have given the company a better edge. They may have brought in new customers or analyzed old paradigms in new and valuable ways. But they don't fit into the rules and expectations of the workplace culture, and they are not delivering results on time.

Can There Be a Better Solution?

You may have noticed that any solution that involves rapid-fire thinkers must include the overall vision and goals of the project and the part they will play. They need to be able to check in with the project manager and feel free to ask questions. They need deadlines and accountability. Many of them will need coaching in order to learn the rules for planning, preparation, task management, and completion of a project by the due date.

When I present seminars to decision-makers about how to work effectively with rapid-fire thinkers, I often hear a familiar theme. "We tried everything. Nothing worked, and we just had to let the person go." During the first hour or so of the seminar, I allow them to vent about these employees who keep making the same mistakes and don't listen. They talk about how agonizing it is to have group meetings with them. Then I read off a list of traits commonly associated with high performers. I ask each person there to make a check mark next to any trait that they believe belongs to any of their difficult employees. When I reach the end of the list, I acknowledge not only that these traits belong to high performers but that they are also commonly held traits of people with ADHD. Usually there is a short silence followed by some embarrassed laughter. Many supervisors or managers haven't thought about their difficult employees in such a positive light. And some of them may see for the first time how these traits may also apply to themselves. That's a good thing when it creates a better understanding and compassion for these challenging workers. Although they came to the seminar to learn a few new management tricks for those folks who drive them crazy, they leave realizing that what they learned today will improve their own ability to be better leaders. They report they are leaving with more understanding of rapid-firing thinkers and a host of new techniques and tools to support and engage these workers more as valuable assets than liabilities of questionable worth.

My message is that everybody wins when we take the time to listen to and learn from one another, especially in the workplace. We have all known individuals who may not be fully aware of their actions and how they adversely affect others on the job. We may have been one of them at some point. We also know how it feels to know what we're doing isn't working; however, we either don't know how to change it, or we are afraid of being laughed at if we ask for help. Almost all of the people I have worked with through the years have wanted to stop their unproductive and destructive behavior patterns but have lacked caring and compassionate help from others. Granted, they often don't seek out the help in the right way and at the right time. But the stories they tell do point out a certain callousness toward them. In my training and seminars, I teach people how to call someone out on his or her behavior in a positive and affirming way, sending the message, "I believe in you and know you can do better. Let's work on this together."

Transforming Workplace Habits of Innovator Brain Types

After we have established that strong performers share the same traits that rapid-fire thinkers have and that taking the time to understand and support rapid-fire thinkers creates a long-term payoff, we settle down into the nuts and bolts of how to turn a downward spiral into an upward swing for our innovator brain types.

Before we decided what sort of strategies and approaches work best, we first have to define the main behaviors of workers with innovator brains. We know that once managers have the tools and strategies to help them interact with their rapid-fire thinkers, they can begin to view these employees as gifts rather than problems.

Characteristics of Innovators in the Workplace

Firstly we may hear that these individuals may not be good at communicating with team members and may actually do better with one-to-one conversations.

Secondly they may have time and task-management difficulties, and they may not get things completed on time or even get to work on time.

Often they are poor at getting help when they need it. Becoming distracted may cause them to miss instructions and key elements of a project, but they are too embarrassed to admit it.

Finally they may exhibit problems with organization in the work environment, which may make it difficult for them to stick with and deliver on priorities. They often find themselves wasting time on the computer.

Oftentimes I hear managers say that they don't want to do "too much handling" of their employees. They tell me that it's not their job, and besides, they don't have the time. In all fairness, managers and supervisors can sometimes feel trapped in their positions because they are often asked to do a lot with limited resources and without much experience in understanding and working with rapid-fire thinkers. I respond that the choice to help the employees structure their roles within the company may be an easier decision than they think, especially when you compare that effort to spending time and money hiring someone else with fewer qualifications and less potential. The following is a workable plan for those who manage and support innovator brain types in the workplace, people ranging from top executives to low-level employees.

Recommendations for Supervisors of Rapid-Fire Thinkers

Strategy 1

When you have employees who are not meeting time and task deadlines, look closely at the circumstances under which they are failing to communicate. Perhaps you need to sit down with them and say, "We need to look at how you are maintaining your deadlines. It looks like you may be having trouble with managing your tasks. Let's talk about how you're structuring your time at work." Guide the employee in establishing daily goals and deadlines and have them report on smaller deadlines. For example, if the project description is due on Monday, the outline of tasks needs to be completed on Tuesday, and the draft proposal should be received no later than Thursday. Since it is challenging for them to manage tasks and time living in the moment as they do, this strategy will provide a structure for them so they don't wait until the last minute and find they can't finish on time. Complicating the matter even more is the probability that they will likely beat themselves up because they "failed again," and for emotional reasons they may avoid reengaging with the task.

Strategy 2

Hire a coach for the workplace. It is most effective and oftentimes necessary to hire an external coach (such as an ADHD coach) because internal coaches typically do not have the expertise to work with this brain type. In particular, an ADHD coach is able to win the executive or employee over through the coach's ability to quickly understand the challenges the person is facing. These coaches are able to get to the problem faster and solve it more quickly, which also saves the company time and money.

Strategy 3

It can be helpful for people to direct the rapid-fire thinkers to supportive services that already exist within the company or workplace. These possibilities could include the Employee Assistance Professional Association (EAPA) or the human resources department. Even though both of these offices are equipped to work with employees and administrative personnel, it is important to make sure that the person assigned to work with the rapid-fire thinker understands the way the innovator brain type works, or the help may not be effective. I find that one of the more disregarded needs in corporate and business environments are trained personnel who understand the needs of different types of workers and their functioning and learning styles, and usually the workers with innovator brains get the least amount of understanding and support.

Strategy 4

Building a better relationship with their bosses is key. And since as we know it takes two to tango, it can be helpful for the boss to set up a conference appointment with the employee to discuss the issues long *before* the performance review takes place and closer to the time when the issues are identified. Begin the conference pointing out the person's strengths and talents and what the boss appreciates about them. That will make it easier for both the boss and the employee or executive to talk about the areas that need improvement. Then it is highly recommended that the boss and employee create a plan for specific expectations and a list of the strategies to achieve them in writing. Finally meeting together *regularly* for a few minutes to check in and see how things are going is critical for the plan to succeed. The great news is that since this strategy is effective at teaching the employees how to manage their time and tasks in the future, they will not require the degree of oversight from their bosses, because they will have learned new time and task-management skills.

I have seen executives and employees with the innovator brain type who have been able to not only retain their positions and enhance their productivity but also become more resilient and valuable contributors to their companies when they are given this structure and support.

Understanding The Innovator Brain Employee's Perspective

Often when bosses approach employees and want to discuss their performances, the employees may initially feel defensive and worried that they are in store for some bad news. If they are rapid-fire thinkers, it is even more likely they have experienced the same thing in regards to the same issues over and over again. Feelings of failure and fear will likely crop up and make it difficult for the employees to hear what their bosses have to say, including critical information about what specifically needs to change and how the employees need to change it.

Before people can change a behavior, they have to be aware of the specific behaviors that are being questioned. But remember, they will likely take feedback personally. They will feel as if their flaws are permanent reflections of them. For this reason, a good way for bosses to approach rapid-fire thinkers is to let them know that it is understandable they are in their present positions. After all, they were not given the insights they needed to do any differently. They are doing things the only way they know how, but they have the capacity to change. When the innovator brain type feels understood and accepted, they hear the message that we value them and want to help. Getting help with changing behavior and developing strategies rather than being labeled inadequate or ineffective is a game changer for this worker. So it's important to remember that when you're working with rapid-fire thinkers, the main idea should read as follows: "It's not you that needs to be fixed. It's not that you are incompetent. It's just that your behaviors and work strategies are out of alignment with your capability. Once we get that figured out, better results will follow."

Comparisons among workers are bad ideas not only because they serve to deflect what needs to be done to solve the problem but because they can also be very damaging. Both rapid-fire thinkers and their bosses are guilty of comparing productivity and performance to other workers and then using that as evidence of substandard work. This can be damaging to the employees' belief they can improve their performance. It could signal them to use their survival instincts and their only remaining option. They will likely hide their flaws, stop trying, and go into avoidance and denial modes, which are the main culprits in bad performance.

We know that rapid-fire thinkers don't need strict employers who evaluate every move and govern through shame and blame. Rather they do best with organized, structured bosses who are able to believe in their potentials. Often our workplace replicates our family of origin. Why? Because we recreate with our thoughts and habits the problems we still need to resolve from our past. Through thought patterns and habits of thinking, we find and attract to us these unresolved issues. They create a very large dissonance inside of us that we are compelled to resolve in any way we can. This is the reason that people suffer workplace trauma without understanding why it happens to them. My own therapist worked with me to understand how my boss reminded me of unresolved issues with my mother and how trying to get along with a specific member of my team mirrored unresolved problems with my father.

Why is this? We bring these experiences into our lives in order to work on them with others in our quest to find peace within ourselves. But we are often unconscious when we do this, and hence, we can feel victimized in our workplaces. What happens as a result is that we cannot meet the expectations that define our job descriptions because we fail to communicate with those around us effectively, positively, and fairly. Because of lacking confidence in our abilities to succeed, we compare ourselves to others that we perceive as more competent. Our energy goes into protecting ourselves from getting hurt and keeping others from discovering we are so flawed. And it all started with perhaps one unresolved issue with a parent, sibling, or other important person in our life!

Here are some affirmations to change this habit of thinking:

- "I choose to create my life in my way because that is my birthright."
- "I have the ability, strength, and courage to make this better."
- "I can change things whenever I set my mind to it."
- "I choose myself rather than rejecting myself."
- "I choose success over failure."

Alice's Story

Alice came to see me when she was on the verge of being fired. Her boss had been given a lot more to do, and he had passed his extra responsibilities onto her. Unfortunately Alice (with her ADHD brain) became overwhelmed and found her compensating mechanisms insufficient. After she received two bad performance reviews, Alice gave me a call.

During our first sessions, Alice learned that the minute she began to feel overwhelmed, she needed to get help right away. Most of her past issues, we discovered, were a result of her fear of asking for help. I shared with her the fact that for innovator brain types, being overwhelmed usually led to more and bigger mistakes and eventually to an inability to recoup what has been lost. So over the course of the next four weeks, in order to combat her overwhelmed state, we worked to lay out her tasks, find the problem areas, come up with new solutions, and establish strategies to support her progress. Because Alice was determined and driven to prove her boss wrong, she asked her boss for a few more weeks to implement what she was learning from her new job coach before he took any further action.

Some of Alice's most effective new workplace behaviors included finding the people already at her place of employment who could help her. She also needed to keep a running record throughout the day of her tasks and the amount of time needed to complete each one in order of priority. When she met with her boss, she could then share her records so that he could see exactly how she was using her time and why it took as long as it did for her to complete her responsibilities.

Her boss was taken aback with the facts in front of him and immediately became willing to work with her to make her daily routines and projects more manageable. Suddenly Alice and her boss had formed a new partnership.

Alice began to regularly tell her boss when she needed help and why. She was outstanding in her ability to apply the insights she was getting from coaching. There are other ways to address the same or similar situations as the one in which Alice found herself. Some of my clients will ask their bosses to tell them which of their behaviors are the most unwanted. They then bring me this information, and together we devise strategies and solutions to address each problem individually. They open up a recurring dialogue with their managers about what they are doing to address each issue and try to report the progress they are making. Like Alice's boss, many supervisors are willing to give additional chances to dedicated employees who are intentional and specific about how they will improve their performances.

You Feel You Are at the Breaking Point

When an innovator's work situation is at the breaking point, the best question to ask is this: "What are the problem behaviors that irritate and worry the manager the most?" Then the employee and I devise a plan to make sure that the boss continues to regularly see consistent progress on those particular behaviors.

But what if you can't create a working relationship with your boss no matter what, either because it is too late and that ship has sailed or because of a personality conflict that can't be overcome. If this is the case, it is important to bring a mentor coach into the picture to determine what is best. Should the innovator leave the job voluntarily rather than risk getting fired? Or should the person remain at his or her place of employment by brokering a deal to move to another department or change supervisors.

When the Computer Is a Minefield

A destructive form of what we often refer to as self-medication is the computer. Self-medicating is finding a way to take the pressure off and take a break from stress for a while. It can take many forms, including smoking marijuana, but typically at work it centers around the computer, tablet, or smartphone. With its games, interactive sites, and video distractions, the computer is a strong stimulus for many rapid-fire thinkers. My clients get caught in the web of this distraction at times to their detriment. That is mainly because they lose track of time while they are interacting with their devices. We call this hyper-focusing. The result could be catastrophic. A brief distraction can go wrong, and one little break can lead to an hour or more of lost time. Then the worker is in trouble. What's even more debilitating is the fact that this behavior can quickly become a habit. Innovator brain types will need to learn to stop all nonwork-related computer use because of their difficulties in managing the behavior. To do this, they must first build awareness of how much time they actually spend on this distraction. Then I ask them to look at the cost of the work they are not completing when they are messing around on their computers. People are usually amazed at how much time they spend not completing work tasks, and they become motivated to turn this behavior around.

Jesse's Story

Jesse is a thirty-four-year-old college-educated man working in the financial industry. He has a job where there is no supervision, yet he is asked to produce projects on his own that require a good deal of planning, interviewing, communicating, and keeping deadlines. Jesse unconsciously gets consistently lost in cyberspace for hours at a time, unaware he is failing to perform his job duties. When Jesse finally woke up and realized his random computer usage was causing him to forget what he was doing and fall further and further behind in his work, he became aware of the toll this behavior was taking and the trouble he was in.

Unfortunately he was also afraid he would look stupid if he asked questions or admitted he had forgotten details. He tried hiding his confusion, but he couldn't. He was about to receive another unsatisfactory performance review, which meant he could be fired in three weeks. This is when Jesse came to me for help.

I asked him if he thought he could buy some more time at work while we sorted through his issues and he began to take control of them. He said no. I could see that a lot of fear had settled into Jesse. The first thing Jesse and I did was arrange an appointment so that he could see his psychiatrist and get back on the medication he had been taking when he was in high school and college. Jesse and I both agreed he could have tried this long ago when he began having trouble with staying on task at work. We hoped since it had worked for him in the past, it would work for him again when he most needed it. Basing our objectives on his two previous performance reviews, we then rolled up our sleeves and went to work. At the end of four sessions, he had a plan. We practiced and practiced how he would present his new goals and the strategies to achieve them. When he had developed enough confidence to lay out his new plan in front of his boss, it was the day before his performance review.

His boss looked at the plan and said, "This sounds good. It's inspiring that you came up with all of this, but I don't see how you will be able to change the way you do things so quickly."

Jesse looked him in the eyes and said, "I promise you I will do this, or you can fire me." I was stunned. Where had Jesse found the guts to promise such a thing? One could say that's the potential of the human spirit. We all have it in us, but not all of us find it and use it.

Jesse had put himself on the line. Wanting very much to support Jesse's courage and the brave stand he had taken, I made sure Jesse and I had a plan to work together for the next three weeks. We had to make sure Jesse could show his boss he could change. In the meantime, Jesse's doctor put him back on the medication he used to take, and Jesse began to report he could feel the difference in his ability to stay focused with fewer distracting episodes.

Jesse continued to make amazing improvements, and while I'd like to say he was able to save his position, he could not. At the end of the story, Jesse did find the mountain was a little too steep to climb. There wasn't enough time to learn and practice the skills he had been neglecting for so long. But because of his courage and the impression he made on his boss—at least in regards to what he *was* able to accomplish—Jesse did not lose his job. He was transferred to another area of the company, where the structure and oversight was more in line with his present level of skills. Although it felt like a demotion and his salary took a dip, Jesse learned a lot from this experience, not the least of which was a belief and confidence in himself he never knew he could have. I believe Jesse now has a better future ahead of him.

The work I did with Jesse is the same work you and I are doing together in this book. We are looking at your skills and talents and what you can do to express them confidently and successfully. Just like you will need to do, my work with Jesse held him accountable to his daily routines.

Is Getting Fired a Death Sentence?

Being fired from a job carries with it the kind of emotional fallout that can feel similar to being rejected by one's own family. It is demoralizing, and it can crush our confidence. At first we may need time to lick our wounds and talk with a professional to keep a positive perspective to the best of our ability. Soon, however, it is important to not remain discouraged and beaten and to move to the next step of getting another job. It's then that I encourage my clients to work with me to see how they coauthored the situation. What part did they play in what went wrong? I tell them that when they can honestly own their part in what happened, they're empowered to do things differently next time so they don't find themselves in the same position again. What did they learn from their experiences that will make them better and more empowered in the future?

Most people cannot see how they are perpetuating their own problems. Coaching is a dispersant. With professional help, rapid-fire thinkers can dislodge the poisonous thoughts and perceptions in their minds and create healthy thinking habits.

It's an important reminder that you can't wait until right before you are about to be fired to get help. As Jesse's story demonstrates, it could be too late by then. Get help at the first sign of trouble and save your confidence, your self-image, and your job. Or you will need to hire a coach to help you move on to another job or career where you are happier and fulfilled.

Being a rapid-fire thinker in a job that is wrong for you is an accident waiting to happen. Rapid-fire thinkers like to be stimulated. Boredom and a lack of real challenge can turn them into stimulation-seeking missiles that are often pointed in a direction opposite to completing work tasks. Employees matched to the wrong jobs don't have to be a disaster if they decide to turn their situations into opportunities to learn what they have been blind to. We all have blind spots, and often we don't learn what they are until disaster strikes. There are no accidents. Life is a learning experience, and we learn many of our more important lessons through mistakes and failures. Unfortunately some people would rather be unhappy in a job than fail at finding a better one. This is where hiring a coach to help them navigate their way through the process makes them more likely to succeed at finding a job that is a better match for their styles.

Many people suffer from not finding their true purposes in life. As we will talk about later, finding our identities, values, purposes, and visions has a great deal to do with the level of happiness and self-fulfillment we will be able to achieve.

The Innovator Gift

Innovators have a higher-than-average ability to solve problems, and this makes them ideal employees during a time of global expansion. What we find instead, however, is many of them struggle to avoid being marginalized and fired. When employers and managers make the extra effort to talk to and understand rapid-fire thinkers, their support and beliefs can empower innovators to change unwanted behaviors. Rapid-fire thinkers can learn to set goals and meet deadlines. They will, however, need the highly structured support and attention from their supervisors to gain control over their workplace challenges. However, the payoff in resilient and inspired innovator employees will be well worth the time and trouble.

CHAPTER 11

Creating a Love that Lasts

Marriage with an ADHD partner can be passionate, exciting, and fulfilling, but sometimes it can be frustrating and alienating. I have saved dozens of relationships with ADHD innovator brain types over the years, and each time I try to put an end to the cycle of frustration and pave the way for real intimacy. This is about authentic, sustainable intimacy. We must identify the challenges to intimacy and learn how to heal the relationship patterns that underlie our more important relationships.

Top Three Practices of Successful ADHD-Labeled Couples

Today it is more important than ever to learn good strategies so that we can have meaningful relationships. With the all-out demands on our time and energy, we can easily neglect what it takes to keep our love for our romantic partner and communication with him or her central where it belongs. All you have to do is look around you at the quality of the relationships you see. You can't help but notice that with many couples, especially after kids come along and careers develop, communication loses its loving edge or takes a backseat to everything else. Romance and sex go into hiding, and before you know it, you wonder where the relationship went.

So here is what I have learned from the couples I have coached with ADHD about what it takes to keep the love alive. I have listed them in rank order beginning with what is most important.

1) Set up consistent romantic practices that you both will keep no matter what. These can be things like date nights, weekends away, romantic vacations for just the two of you, time in the evening and on the weekend to relax with each other, etc. Even with the arrival of children, even with career pressures, even with the fear and stress of life in the 21st century, it is critical that you always keep consistent romantic practices a top priority if you want your relationship to stay on track.

2) Routinely talk out and resolve issues. Do this at least once a week. Avoid building resentments. Then go out and celebrate. This routine will make it easier to keep communication from becoming negative and angry. When you know you will be sitting down to discuss things in a few days, you can keep track of what you're unhappy about and avoid building up a pile of anger and frustration. This practice will help partners not build up resentment, which is the single main reason people fall out of love and eventually get divorced. Get a babysitter, have your "business meeting," and then go out to dinner, a movie, or the theater. Celebrate your hard work and successful outcomes.

3) Get support from friends, relatives, and professionals Research tells us that ADHD and other couples who have a network of support from extended family and friends get more helpful feedback as well as more support to stay together and work things out. They also have more opportunity to

share exclusive time for each other. Additionally, ADHD couples often require professional help from an established ADHD couples coach or ADHD couples therapist because of potential additional strain on the relationship from untreated or unaddressed ADHD. Many couples have reported that getting into coaching or therapy at the first sign of a problem makes all the difference.

At the beginning I often hear a lot of reasons why couples can't do these things. These people tell me that they don't have the time, that they don't have the money, that they're too tired, that they can't get a babysitter, that it won't help, that it's too late, and that their spouse won't go to therapy. I tell them they can have reasons or they can have results. If they're not working to stay together, then they are most assuredly working to come apart. Whether or not they have consciously chosen to stay or leave the relationship, being willing to let go of the need to be the one who is right – making their spouse the one who is wrong - is choosing to bring their partner back into a loving relationship. The opposite also applies. Not being willing to defer ego gratification is choosing to give up.

Of course, when it comes to staying in or leaving your relationship, the sooner the most important questions are asked, the better for everyone. Here are the most critical questions people can ask in order to move away from confusion and negativity in their relationships and toward making a healthy decision:

1. On a scale of one to ten, how important is it to keep your relationship/family together?
2. What are you willing to change to keep the family together?
3. What action are you initially willing to take to get the ball rolling?

So how do you determine what your answers mean? If your answer to the first question is five or less, if you're unwilling to be first to initiate significant changes on your own without promises of the same from your partner, and if you cannot see yourself taking bold action without guarantees, what do you think your chances are of saving your relationship?

There's some good news. In my experience those couples who engage in even one of the practices outlined previously can expect a better chance of making it over the long term.

If your relationship is not working out the way you want or is seriously in trouble, you might want to consider the value of the three key practices previously outlined that many couples feel have saved or are saving their relationships. Hopefully you have awakened and become conscious enough to see that you do have the choice to stay or to go, that there really are things you can do to save your relationship, and that if you use these key practices, you will be able to make good decisions for yourself and for everyone involved. What if the reason you're reading this book is so you can stop suffering and struggling and get on with your life? How will your decision to fish or cut bait in your relationship give you the opportunity to reclaim a life of love, purpose, and happiness?

I wish you the best outcome you are capable of, and I will remind you that it is of the utmost importance that this work comes more from your heart and less from your head!

Love and Intimacy with an Innovator Brain Type

So you feel you are in love with someone who has the innovator type brain. You're coming up on four and a half years of marriage, and every time you get in the shower or start to drive the car, you start crying. You realize you're depressed, but every time you try to discuss your feelings and frustrations with your innovator partner, he or she becomes defensive and argues. Your partner tunes you out, or shuts down and becomes emotionally unavailable. Sound familiar?

Couples with the innovator brain type have the same problems as other couples, communication issues being chief among them. The main difference between the two is that innovators bring a particular type of emotional baggage to their relationships because of past issues when they were growing up and not feeling understood or supported. Members of these couples are afraid to ask for what they need for fear they won't get it, they don't deserve it, or they can't trust themselves to reciprocate. They lack confidence in their abilities to meet the expectations of others, including their own mates. It is important to understand what is going on in your relationship from the point of view of the innovator.

Being in a relationship with an innovator is full of ups and downs. When conflicts occur, they can be even harder to resolve because of deep-seated feelings and painful memories these partners bring to the relationship. On the other hand, an innovator can bring bouquets of smiles, new experiences and adventures, new perspectives on old themes, and often an open, loving heart. It can definitely be worth the effort to find a way to communicate better with your innovator partner. Building trust and affection can be hard work, but for many people it is definitely worth the effort.

Blurting, arguing, and not paying attention can hurt and cause you to feel your partner does not love or respect you. In fact, innovator brain types are used to others abandoning them because of these same behaviors. In relationships, however, one of the partners gets to know a charming, intelligent, and fun person, but gradually that person discovers that the other can act like an immature and resistant teenager at times. These people find themselves waiting for an e-mail, call, or ride that never comes. They want to spend time with their innovator partners, but their partners don't want to talk and quickly make haste to the computer. They make simple requests for help, but the innovator partners forget and do not act remorseful. The innovator partners make promises to change, but frustratingly the same cycle keeps repeating over and over again.

There is a big payoff to having innovators in your life. They're fun and creative thinkers and good problem solvers, and they're highly successful, caring, and compassionate people. Many people become motivated and willing to change their behaviors once they see clearly and become confident enough that they believe there's actually a way to change their behaviors. People will need patience and ADHD coaching to turn this situation around. Your job is to not give up on them or yourself.

Miranda's Story

Miranda, my coaching client of three years, has a marriage that has remained intact. As an innovator, Miranda learned how to put another bead on her string of self-control, self-awareness, and self-love one day at a time. Her hard work and dedication to creative problem solving with her partner has paid off with a better relationship. Miranda learned that she could have the benefits of being an innovator and still be able to smooth out the rough edges that come with it.

Miranda was an innovator with traits that contributed to her multiple strengths, but these also contributed to some important issues that were continually angering and upsetting her husband. Miranda forgot to do the things she and her husband agreed to do. She would spend long hours at work and lose track of time. She would miss dinner, and when she did get home, she spent extra time with the children, interrupting their bedtime routines. Her husband accused her of needing everything her way and he told her that he felt like an afterthought. He yelled at her when they got into arguments. He was sick and tired of holding down the fort at home while she lived life any way she chose and on her terms. He wanted out of the marriage and didn't believe things could be fixed because he believed Miranda couldn't change.

How did she do it? Miranda did not do it alone. Miranda went into counseling to find out how she was contributing to her poor relationship with her partner by understanding her own life and past family history. This was no easy task. After all, at the same time that she was attempting to do the hard work of learning from her past what she could do to save her relationship in the present, her husband consistently reacted to her in anger. Miranda was very worried about her three children (ages two to eleven), and she felt physically overwhelmed and emotionally drained. For them she continued to do her best to put on a happy face and keep her composure.

Miranda was able to finally convince her husband to go to therapy with her. But she never knew when he would accompany her or not. After four months with limited success, Miranda and her husband were able to achieve a truce. They stopped being angry and aggressive with each other. Exhausted and fed up, they decided to separate.

That was when Miranda heard about me from a colleague, and she decided to give me a call. After Miranda and I talked about the possibilities of what ADHD couples coaching could potentially do for them, she decided it was promising enough to give it one last try. Although it wasn't easy, Miranda managed to convince her husband to come to four appointments, and then he would be free to make up his mind about whether he wanted to continue or not.

As it turned out, Miranda and her husband were able to commit to long-term coaching, and they kept it up for eighteen months. Yes, it was a tough road, and yes, there were constant disappointments along the way. But to their credit, Miranda and her husband did not give up, and as a result, they were able to carve out a new relationship for themselves so that they could keep their marriage together.

Always treat your partner like you would want him or her to treat you. When you reach out to your partner and make it about him or her first and you second, you are acknowledging you care about them. Then you have taken the first real step toward working through the issue. That kind of caring attention will help you keep misunderstandings and resentments in check. That way they won't build up into larger problems. Living with the ADHD label in this society can be lonely and fearful. People with this label can find it difficult to get close to others out of fear they will be rejected. Taking responsibility instead of blaming your innovator partner will get you far. When people actually care enough to reach out and gently communicate the truth with respect and love, innovators have the opportunity to respond positively and in collaboration with others.

Some innovators are very motivated to change their behaviors. Some are not ready to change. And others are driven to succeed but are not good at listening to and accepting ideas and feedback. Whatever the case, it is important to remember that people with this brain type will require our respect, acceptance, and a belief that they have something valuable to offer. People with the rapid-fire thinking trait usually have a low awareness of how they come across to others, including their partners. They need people to give them feedback in a loving and caring way. It has been my experience that with this approach, even the most resistant innovators can be won over. They will start believing that they, too, can change with help.

Innovators experience a considerable amount of rejection in their childhoods and their teen years because they don't fit in. They break rules inadvertently and come across as less interested in the important things like school performance and helping out at home. They seem more interested in engaging in self-gratifying pursuits like games and technology. No one told them that the reason for their ill-placed sense of importance was the constant failure of not living up to the expectations of school and home. When you keep failing and don't understand why and have no one to guide you, your only option is to shut down your emotions and look for activities that can act as diversions from unrelenting failure. Whatever the case, many rapid-fire thinkers never learned how to engage in the trusting sorts of relationships that lead to intimacy.

Unfortunately when you shut down your emotions, you shut down your ability to respond effectively. This puts you at further risk of doing, speaking, and behaving in the wrong way. People want to get close to you but complain that they can't find an opening and they eventually give up trying. You see their behaviors as further acknowledgment that you are not worthy or good enough. And it can go on like that unless something intervenes.

Loving communication in the key to unlocking your innovator's defenses. Innovators can be afraid or ashamed to ask for help. Rapid-fire thinkers want desperately to open up their emotional world, but they don't have the key, which is trust. Many rapid-fire thinkers are quick to make negative assessments of the situation and blame themselves. This gives them an even harder mountain to climb—at least in their eyes. Communication is difficult when it means making oneself vulnerable to another. It can be difficult to cross into trust, to reach out fearlessly and to share oneself. Rapid-fire thinkers can feel more insecure than their counterparts. Here are seven of the ways that an innovator brain type avoids intimacy either consciously or unconsciously:

- They are interested in the experience only. They stay focused on the fun and interesting things they do with their partners and avoid emotional involvement.

- They may choose unavailable people. They pursue relationships with people who are unavailable for any serious commitment because they are addicted, troubled, married, or otherwise not going to work out.

- They are ready to leave when it gets uncomfortable. They avoid participating in emotionally open discussions, hoping that their partners will not insist on more disclosure, and they are ready to walk away if their partners do require more.

- They may isolate themselves. They confine their relationships to those that are basic to survival, (i.e., their connections to their boss, their mailmen, their doctors, their bankers, etc.).

- They often use technology as a *friend*. They tell themselves that interacting with people online is the same as having real emotionally intimate relationships.
- They pretend to share intimacy. They make up stories and express feelings in order to fit in and be a part of a group or a relationship without taking any real risk.
- They consistently use distracters (such as sex, anger, arguments, physical pain, personal problems, projects, and their jobs) to distance themselves from open discussions about their needs and feelings.

Good News

The good news is that we're rapid-fire thinkers! That means that if we do decide to ask for help, we're going to tackle the problem and solve it faster and better than a person who isn't a rapid-fire thinker. What a relief! All we have to do is acknowledge that we have a problem and that we need help. We have to be ready to change, but what's that compared to the years of feeling alone, denigrated, and isolated? In a therapeutic and/or coaching relationship, innovators learn to value themselves and appreciate their strengths and what they bring to their relationships. They learn to trust themselves and trust other people. Learning to trust clears the fog away so that they can see what they've been missing, namely the concern and interest that the other person holds for them.

As rapid-fire thinkers, we face the fear that someone will hurt us. Finally asking for and receiving help allows rapid-fire thinkers the opportunity to stop taking things personally and see themselves as worthwhile human beings. Now when they interact with others, they can see clearly that these people are just making suggestions, not saying, "You are wrong again. Will you ever get it right?"

We all know that we create our reality with our thoughts and by the way we respond to circumstances. When I work with clients who are learning to change their ways of thinking, I often hear them say, "It's just so hard not to go into defensive counterattacks." It is hard to stop this lurch into combat. You will need a helping partner to see you through it. But it can be done. I see it happen every day. People let down their guards and learn to love and trust themselves with the help of coaches or therapists.

The first question I ask my clients when I am dealing with this issue is this: "What's your earliest memory of not being able to connect with someone emotionally?" We then reinterpret their histories to determine what it was that caused them to respond reactively and defensively. Do they remember their first experiences of rejection? We talk about how they built a history of rejection around some early incidents that were reinforced over time. Now they have the opportunity to go back in time and look at how that happened. They can reinterpret their histories with a more accurate understanding. When we are able to replay and reinterpret experiences from our past with someone's help, we can begin to see a new reality. It can be such a relief to go back and see that we were not stupid and incompetent. The truth is that we just didn't understand why we couldn't fit in, and we felt incapable of doing something about it back then.

When you realize your self-worth, you get to ask yourself, "What possibilities are available to me now?" Now you have the opportunity to build a better relationship with a partner. You can begin to explore new relationship possibilities together and take on new roles that work better for you.

When conflicts arise—and they always do—give your partner the benefit of the doubt. Because your partner loves you, you can assume that you two will work the problem out. You both have to believe in your relationship though.

By now most people know the value of using "I" messages. "I feel this." "I heard you say this." "I believe you mean this." Those are much different than accusatory statements. "You always do this." "You make me feel bad." "I" statements will leave the door open for continued dialogue and avoid putting the other person on the defensive. Other great phrases are those that indicate you are curious about what the other person is thinking or how your partner is feeling. For example, you may ask, "So what is it I do that annoys you?"

Often when rapid-fire thinkers ask what is annoying their partners, they hear this reply: "You're constantly getting distracted when I'm talking to you." A helpful response could be as follows: "I see how that can be annoying. It's not that I'm not interested in what you have to say. I'm just distracted by what is going on around me right now. Can we find another time or place to talk about this?" This is a proactive and affirming way they can let their partners know what the difficulty is from their points of view.

Learning how to respond with emotional openness can happen inside of a coaching relationship. Each opportunity to communicate comes under the scrutiny of the client and his or her coach. Like a machine with moving parts, the client's life is slowly disassembled, and each supposition, choice, and action is analyzed. Gradually the clients will develop greater insights into the causes and effects of their own behaviors and learn new ways of being emotionally available to themselves and to others.

Many couples want their partnerships to work. They want to fix them when they are broken, but these people don't realize that it is the intimacy they don't have with *themselves* that is preventing their loving relationships from working. You must put your own house in order before you can put your relationship house in order.

The couples I work with gradually begin to see their negative patterns and what each person is doing to keep the patterns going. The typical scenario is when one person is the perpetrator, and the other is the victim. The perpetrators get angry because they aren't getting what they need, and consequently they lash out at their partners. Their partners get angry, and they fight back by emotionally checking out withholding affection from the perpetrators. In couples coaching, we work to recognize how each person's behavior reinforces the other person's behavior through blaming. The "it's not my fault" reaction happens when someone does not see the role he or she is playing that keeps the pattern going. It's not possible to listen and have empathy when you're busy defending yourself.

Here is an example of a more positive scenario where listening to your partner can begin to open doors instead of close them:

John says, "I'm angry and hurt, Karen! And now you're going to tell me I shouldn't be feeling this way."

Karen says, "You have the right to feel that way, John."

John says, "What do you mean?"

Karen says, "I mean I hear you."

In this case, Karen is learning how to avoid the need to defend herself in conflicts with John. Through our work, she has begun to see that the way in which she has been communicating cuts off John's desire to talk openly with her. Karen's job is to see how she can become a more responsive and caring partner through better attempts to listen and understand. In turn, this will create a desire in her partner to do the same, paving the way to better outcomes.

As I work with couples, it can sometimes become a challenge to make sure that each person leaves feeling hopeful. I make an effort to manage each session so that both parties feel that hope, but sometimes the couple will need to go the extra distance between sessions.

Usually innovators have felt deeply disappointed in themselves and the fact they are constantly letting others down. It's important for them to feel that they can do better even though typically their partners feel that their innovator counterparts are not pulling their weight in the relationship. In the beginning of couples coaching, people can often have blind spots about how they are contributing to the conflicts. Often they come to sessions and won't talk to one another. I start off by saying to them, "No one is sure this is going to work. Let's all agree that we'll let that expectation go and just agree to be loving and supportive of each other during this session." After they learn how to look closely and openly at themselves and each other, they begin to report some good things that happened during the week that will contribute to some future breakthroughs. If they stay with it, many couples can begin to transform their perspectives toward their relationships. They become more aware of what they brought into the relationship from their own past that is getting in the way of good communication in the present. They can see how their own wounds are also roadblocks and quickly realize that they need to work on themselves first. Then they can begin to heal their current relationships.

Change like this in a loving relationship requires that each person take responsibility for what they are contributing to the conflict. Coaching typically takes less time than the traditional model of therapy because it is task and action-oriented. These faster turnaround times can often save relationships that are at their breaking points. At the end of each session, I ask my innovator clients, "How is this working for you? Is there anything we can do differently or better?" In addition to asking for valuable feedback, it is my intention to model for them the behavior and communication practices I am attempting to teach them.

When rapid-fire thinkers are ready to say, "Hey, I need a little help," then they have just stepped into transformation mode. With some help from coaches and mentors, they can begin to unpackage old habits, beliefs, and routines and accept a new set of habits, beliefs and routine strategies. Being ready to change can be the biggest change of all. Readiness opens up your heart and your mind. Putting down your shield and embracing your fears can't help but fill you with hope. Here is a poem by one of my favorite poets that describes hope beautifully:

Hope*
Hope is the thing with feathers
That perches in the soul,
And sings the tune—without the words,
And never stops at all,
And sweetest in the gale is heard;
And sore must be the storm

That could abash the little bird
That kept so many warm.
I've heard it in the chillest land,
And on the strangest sea;
Yet, never, in extremity,
It asked a crumb of me.

— Emily Dickenson

CHAPTER 12

Raising an Incredible Innovator

People with ADHD have children with ADHD. Anyone who grew up with the ADHD stigma of the 80s and 90s wants to raise well-adjusted children with their self-confidence intact. From the toddler stage through young adulthood, I will be sharing step by step advice pertaining to good parenting skills, how to advocate for your kids with innovator brains, the best use of the resources around you, and how to encourage your children so that they don't feel like they're struggling alone.

Parenting Innovator Children

When parents don't know how to respond to their innovator children's behavior, conflict and chaos can occur. Not knowing how to control their children, parents become frustrated and angry at themselves. Then they become angry with their children.

Seeing Themselves through Your Eyes

People with the innovator gene typically have a low awareness of how they are coming across to others. As we've discussed, they need feedback to be given in a loving and caring way. It's the same with parenting innovator children. They, too, need us to take the time and make the effort to tell them how their gifts and talents are a contribution to us. Just like innovator adults, children need to learn they have a gifted brain, even though it can be disorganized and unfocused. Once they understand they can learn to manage these issues and receive help from a qualified ADHD coach, they are able to feel okay about themselves and keep their self-esteem intact.

Eugene's Story

Eugene was a fifth-grader who was attending school in a different community from the one in which he lived in order to get a better education. In his first year, he experienced multiple issues because his classmates were ahead of him in almost every academic subject. He was so far behind in his skills that even I entertained the idea he could not make up the distance within a reasonable period of time. His situation was additionally challenging because he felt he did not fit in socially. Plus he didn't feel liked by his teachers.

In spite of the downside to his situation, Eugene, his parents, and I decided to work together to see if we could turn the situation around. Eugene's parents and I agreed it was too soon to throw in the towel and give up, and luckily for us, Eugene was willing to go along with the plan.

Early on we discovered that Eugene was using some behaviors that were thwarting the process. He wanted to do things his way like he was used to doing. After all, it had always worked for him in the past. He was also developing the habit of blaming his teachers and the school for the problems he was having. He didn't see that his stubbornness in adapting to his new school environment and unwillingness to do things in new and different ways were part of the problem. It became clear to his parents and me that if we didn't help Eugene face his behaviors, they would continue to cause him to fail.

Eugene and I worked together once a week to help him understand how his innovator brain worked differently from his classmates' brains. We talked about how the advantages of smarts, creativity, problem solving, and inventiveness would take him far. And then we talked about how he would also be required to learn to manage his impulses and distractions in order to fit within the expectations of school and society. It was hard work. Insights that led to new ways of doing things (e.g., how to plan time and tasks, manage projects, prepare for tests, and complete homework) were slow to happen. Time was ticking away, and Eugene was barely scraping by. Some months went by before we were able to build up Eugene's self-confidence to the point where he was willing to try new things that would lead to changing some unwanted behaviors.

To their credit, his parents understood enough of what was going on to have faith in the process of coaching, which allowed Eugene and me to work together for six years. During that span of time, Eugene painstakingly learned to take the advice of teachers, counselors, and tutors and use that advice and encouragement to improve the way he prepared for tests, completed his homework, reviewed his notes, and managed time and tasks, especially when it came to long-term assignments. And the most difficult hurdle of all for Eugene to get over was his comfort level when he needed to ask for help at the first sign of trouble.

In the end, Eugene, who so often seemed to be his own worst enemy, fooled us all and even himself. After he graduated from high school, he was accepted into the one of the best music schools in the country, his first choice.

Perhaps Eugene's story serves to illustrate the importance of self-acceptance. When you can accept yourself and how having a rapid-fire thinking brain affects you personally, you will learn to manage it and make the most of its gifts. And speaking of gifts, having the confidence to be yourself and allow those around you to appreciate your true identity is a gift to yourself.

The pain of being different and not fitting in begins in childhood. Children with innovator brains grow up feeling convinced they are stupid. They work very hard not to appear that way at school and in public, and it's an exhausting experience. Children need our understanding, and we need to make sure they get it at home, at school, and in other areas of their lives. To succeed, innovators need to learn to self-advocate early in childhood so that they will know how to get help when and how they need it.

What If Both Parents Have the Innovator Gene?

When parents have ADHD, they can be a drain on their children because of their own denial. I work with many young people who have fathers who don't think they need help. These fathers feel they've been able to cope successfully with their lives. After all, they have high-ranking positions at renowned companies, or they've made a lot of money.

When both of the parents are innovators, it is more complicated and more challenging to get guidance and support because both are experiencing the same or similar challenges. Often when both the husband and wife have an ADHD diagnosis, it can be more chaotic and argumentative in the household, as both are likely struggling with the same or very similar issues.

Parents must understand that they must work on their own relationship issues first before they will be effective at helping and supporting their innovator children. The key to this situation is to get someone else involved. A couples or family ADHD coach should be consulted for guidance with parenting innovator children. An ADHD couples coach can make all the difference because the coach understands how issues with this brain type interact to create the unique problems within innovator households. If you're married, that third person makes it easier to see who owns which issue. It can be hard to see who is responsible for the problems in the household when you're right in the middle and can't see the forest for the trees. As a couple, it is important to realize you will need a coach or counselor on a regular basis until each of you has worked through your issues enough to take responsibility for your own behavior.

When possible, it's great to join a support group for spouses, parents, sons, daughters, or siblings of people with the innovator brain type. Sharing your own experiences with others who have the same or similar experiences will help you feel understood and not alone in your frustration. It may even give you the opportunity to laugh at yourself and release anxiety. People tell me all the time that being in these support groups takes the pressure off, and it's often a relief to hear other people talk about their own frustrations and anger when it comes to living with innovators. It is likely most people in your group will have exactly the same issues. They will share ideas and solutions and help you gain a more favorable perspective on your own situation.

Neurological testing, sometimes referred to as neuropsychological or "neuropsych testing," is another way to go. Some people like the idea of pinpointing exactly how their versions of the innovator brain affects their behaviors because the testing will show levels of functionality in a wide range of areas. You may want more specific information about your strengths and weaknesses and why you do things in certain ways. If so, testing may be a good option for you. The assessment process and feedback from the tester will also help you become clear about how, when, and where to go for help when you need it. Not everyone, however, wants or needs this type of specific and detailed information. Unless it is required for school or work purposes, it isn't necessary.

Books can be another source of good information about innovator brains, even though they may use the old ADHD definition. Valuable things can be learned from other people's personal experiences and there is a wealth of information on helpful strategies, the latest research, and accepted practices relating to innovator brain types. Reading books on ADHD can offer insights and understandings that can alter our thinking in a good way. The more we read and compare different beliefs and points of view, the easier it is for us to make up our own minds about what we feel comfortable with. I always recommend that people search on line at www.Amazon.com, www.BarnesandNoble.com and www.AddWarehouse.com to name 3 popular sites. Then if you can, go to the actual store to leaf through the books you've identified before buying. Different books will appeal to different readers.

The Importance of Delegating Childcare

We've come a long way from the village concept and practice of raising children. It is more common now to have two working parents and single parent homes. Raising children takes energy, patience, and understanding. Raising innovator children takes even more of that. All parents need a break from their children. Having backup help in raising your child allows you to unwind and take some time to rest and care for yourself. Spending long periods of time attempting to manage the behavior of innovator children can be draining and frustrating. You are more likely to snap at your child and do or say things you may regret later. This is a problem I see frequently in my practice, and it must be dealt with accordingly. When the parents make the time for themselves together and separately to get away from the responsibilities of home and family, lining up family members or babysitters to take over childcare responsibilities, families are happier and healthier because parents are happier and healthier.

Medication for yourself and/or your child can also be a great help even when it is not your first choice. Here's a helpful way to consider this option: Weigh the choice of medication for a limited period of time against a lifetime of self-esteem issues because of early school failure.

There were times with my first child when my husband would come home at night and he would find both of us on the floor in a heap of tears. I would hand him the baby and just get in the car and go somewhere. I needed a break. In the old days, there were other people around a new family—maids, nannies, aunties, and grannies. Today's common structure in which the mother and father are the only caregivers doesn't meet the needs of some families. If you have innovator children, consider how to create a balance of work/productivity and fun/rest in your life so that both you and your spouse can be role models for the benefit of your child. Most of us would agree we want to raise strong, resilient, and confident children. To do that, we need to weigh and consider how we nurture the needs of both parents and children within the family constellation.

As a parent, you want options other than resigning yourself to the fact that your child is losing confidence, tuning out, and shutting off. Some children do well with medication while others do not. Some parents are comfortable with their children taking medication while others feel opposed. Most children do make progress as a result of working with ADHD coaches. I encourage parents to join organizations like Children and Adults with Attention Deficit/Hyperactivity Disorder (CHADD.org) to enlist the help of recommended psychologists and coaches and to learn where the best resources are and how they can use them effectively. It will be up to each set of parents to find the right match of professional resources that most effectively help their children.

Having innovator children at home can also be disruptive. It can be a significant source of stress, and at its worst, it can even cause a couple to break up and divorce. I encourage parents of innovator children to get help from professionals, join support groups, talk to other parents with innovator children, learn how to use humor to diffuse situations, and create time and space for each other. Otherwise, these school years can become power struggles and create unhappy memories instead of happy ones. The good thing about innovator children is that they can be more resilient and adaptable than other children. Even though times can be hard and relationships at home can be strained, they usually make it through these years and turn out well, ready to face the world away from home.

Consistency and Structure with Innovator Children

For innovator children, structures and consistency is critical to their successes. Innovator children find it very difficult to stay focused without clear directions and reliable daily academic routines. The innovator brain does not respond to haphazard training. Because of the distracted nature of the brain type, learning takes place with continuous repetition of facts, formulas, and concepts except in any area of great interest to the child. The innovator brain tends to default to what is the most interesting and stimulating and stay with it. That is both the gift and the downside of having an innovator brain. Areas of the curriculum where the children lack interest will not motivate them to pay attention. But if the classroom and teacher are consistent in routines and preparation, innovator children will be able to train their brains to attend. All children thrive on structure. Innovator children require it. Consistent morning routines, set times when they pick out their clothes for school, structured school days and times when they eat dinner, do their homework and go to bed- the more constant and unchanging the daily routine, the easier it is to train the brain to do what is expected.

Children may act like they don't like structure, and the parent will need to enforce that structure for them to reap the benefits of it. Especially with innovator children, the parents will need to lay down the law and stick with it. Children feel safe with reliable parents who don't cave in to pressure or tantrums. This is the way they learn to build their own internal behavior management systems so that they can grow up to be responsible adults. Children who come from structured and moderately strict families appear to understand better how to manage themselves in different situations.

Everybody prospers and benefits from structured environments. Remember that rapid-fire thinking children don't have brains that are naturally developed with structure-building competencies like other kids' brains, so they need a consistent structure put in place for them throughout their childhoods and adolescences. There is a big upside to this, however, because innovator children with well-trained brains will carry that discipline over to adolescence and adulthood.

Charlie's Story

Charlie was a kid who had low self-esteem when he started Boston Latin School in the ninth grade. Boston Latin School is a prestigious exam school attended by high-functioning kids from all over the city. Charlie was used to being the high-functioning kid in his elementary school, but not long after he began the school year, Charlie began to fall behind in the highly competitive environment of BLS. When we met initially, I could see that he hadn't adjusted to losing the structure and the accountability of his previous school environment. Consequently he was quickly losing faith in himself.

We brainstormed ways that he could speed up adapting to his new environment and how he could structure his life in a different way to get his work done on time. By allowing his parents to be part of the coaching process, he created a supporting role for them that did not include persistent intervention in the form of nagging, questioning, and criticizing.

Charlie proved that he was still a smart kid by agreeing to adopt a calendar planning system that helped him schedule everything related to school and included appointments, after-school activities, and unique events. Emphasis was put on making sure Charlie had his homework clearly laid out according to exact assignments and due dates. This new calendar system made it possible for Charlie to manage his time and get more schoolwork done.

It also came out during our discussions that Charlie had not made friends and did not really feel like he was a part of his new school. He feared not being liked. We began to have discussions about why and how he was likable by using evidence from his past school friendships. He began to realize that he could start with one small step to get involved, and so he joined the radio club because he had always had a keen interest in radio announcing. It was hard for Charlie to take that first step, but he stuck with it. After a couple of months, word got around that he was really good at it, and Charlie started making new friends. In time Charlie rose to the rank of school radio broadcaster and became so good at it he was eventually invited to help out with a local cable TV station. His teachers loved what he was doing, and his classmates wanted to be a part of it. People in the community applauded him. This evidence of his competence began to give him the confidence and resilience he needed to feel like a part of his school's culture.

Charlie was able to go from doing poorly in academics during his first year in high school to making the kind of steady progress during the next three years that allowed colleges to determine he was a rising star. After four years Charlie was accepted into one of his top-three college choices.

An important factor in Charlie's success was his parents' willingness to keep supporting the coaching he was getting. Parents sometimes give up too soon. They say, "Coaching isn't working, so let's stop." No matter how much I explain to parents that coaching takes time and that changes must first happen internally before they manifest results externally, they sometimes give up on the process. Charlie's parents allowed him to stay with his coach the first, second, and third year of high school. After three years he was confident and ready to function independently in college.

Including Parents in the Coaching Process

If the child is under the age of twelve, I recommend that parents have a two-way communication with the coach and use a team approach with teachers and other professionals included in the circle of helpers, including psychiatrists, speech or occupational therapists, psychotherapists, and/or social workers. With older children, the ADHD coach can communicate to the parents general improvement milestones without breaking confidentiality with their child. If the children are older than twelve, I suggest they self-report to parents about their progress. However, since not all children that age want to talk openly with their parents, I allow parents to e-mail me their observations so I can use them to get a more complete picture in my work with their children. Additionally, with that age group, I suggest meeting once every six weeks with both parents and children present for the purpose of checking in and determining how things are going. Lastly the students and I sometimes send notes back and forth to their parents. These often state progress and ask for feedback to questions like "Do you notice that I'm doing my homework better?" and "Do you see that I'm not on the Internet and watching TV as much as I used to be?" At the beginning I encourage parents to be patient because it could take a year or longer to accomplish what they want for their children.

In families where at least one parent and one child clearly have the innovator gene, family relationships can be complicated. The innovators feel they are always in the wrong according to the viewpoints of other family members, while these other family members are angry because they feel the innovators constantly let them down. When one or both parents have the innovator brain type, there can be a lot of arguing and condemnation. When one or more children are involved, sibling relationships suffer, parent and child relationships are strained, and the parent's own relationship is constantly being tested. It is easy to see how this situation can create a volatile and frustrating home environment. Unfortunately, families such as this are often reluctant to get help. This is tragic when good coaching can teach families how to understand what is actually happening between them and assist them in developing better ways to get along until the family gets it right. Good coaches teach parents how to reach out to the resources around them for the support they need to maintain healthy relationships. Good coaching ensures that innovator families get the help they need to succeed and thrive.

The Preschool Years

Between the ages of birth and four or five, children separate from their parents and form their identities or their core senses of self. These are critical years for them to get the message that they are loved and capable. In the early years of a child's development, the main challenge for a parent is how to patiently respond to the child so that he or she learns limits without getting any negative messages. When a three-year-old boy can't be still one minute and grabs and throws everything within his reach, it's hard for parents not to find themselves yelling, "No!" numerous times a day. Physically punishing children through spanking, yanking, or slapping may give parents back their power in the moment, but in effect, this teaches the children to be afraid and to feel bad about themselves. Based on the hyperactive nature of some innovator children and the "lost in their own world" nature of other innovator children, it is not hard to understand how well-meaning parents may find themselves in an unrelenting reactive cycle with their innovator children.

Here is a helpful series of steps you can take when you see your little ones circling the dinner table at top speed with forks in their hands. Best of all, this series of steps take seconds to accomplish.

- Take a deep breath and calm yourself.
- Gently restrain the children or ask them to restrain themselves.

- Bend down and look directly into their faces and ask, "How do you feel? What's going on? What do you need?"
- Offer alternatives. "You could climb up to the top of the hill in the backyard and roll down. You can race me down the street, or you could play with your tunnel toy in the playroom."
- Acknowledge the children for their willingness to cooperate.

Let's say that you look out of the window and your five-year-old son is pulling the branches of the neighbor's wisteria tree down and stripping them of leaves. You can call out, "Stop it now!" in a military commando voice, or you can call out, "Sam, please treat the tree gently. Leave the leaves on it." Then when Sam stops pulling the leaves off, it's a good idea to acknowledge it by thanking him for being kind to the tree. You have not only stopped your child's inappropriate behavior, but you have just had an important teaching moment about the values of caring for nature.

However, if Sam ignores you, try again, and if necessary, remove him to a place where you and he can talk without distractions. If he continues to pull the leaves off of the tree, he may need the consequence of a timeout or a loss of privileges. Often the solution is as easy as refocusing Sam with another activity like building a fort in the yard by using lawn chairs and old blankets. Using positive language and actions with children takes more self-control and may take a little more time on the part of the parent, but the benefits are immeasurable for the strength of character and the well-being of your children in the long run.

Gradually as you continue to apply patience and a calm voice, the little innovators will learn to think of alternatives for themselves. They will want to please their parents, other adults, and friends by doing the right thing. They will need a lot of help in the beginning from their parents. Most of all, because they were treated calmly and lovingly during the early years between birth and five and given the message that they were perfectly acceptable just the way they were, it is more likely they will endure the future assaults to their self-esteem that all children must undergo.

In most families parents have unmet needs of their own. There is greater stress these days just trying to keep up with the pace of activity and the demands that are expected of adults in our society. Parents are stressed to the limit with jobs and career expectations, trying to spend quality time with their families and take care of the house, pets, finances, and themselves, which usually falls to the bottom of the priority list. Compounding the situation is the kind of thinking that causes parents to enroll their children in numerous activities for fear they will fall behind the achievements of their peers, and then there's the added stress of the time, money, and transportation back and forth that these activities require. It is no wonder parents are not getting their own needs met individually and as a couple. They have no time left for each other. To me this whole paragraph sounds like a recipe for high emotional stress and angry outbursts between the parents, not to mention between the parents and the children. However, it is up to the adults in this situation to take care of themselves to the best of their abilities by getting help and being responsible for their own mental, emotional, and physical health. Happy parents make for happy children. Unhappy, angry parents make for unhappy, angry children. That's the way it works. The next time you are condemning or being verbally abusive to each other, ask yourselves what is more important. Is your argument, which will soon disappear, as important as the damaging effect it will have on your children for their lifetimes? Instead of taking the easy way, do the right thing. You'll sleep better at night and be a happier person. Love, understanding, and healthy self-esteem are the most important possessions to all human beings. Don't all children deserve that? You get one chance to raise them. Do it right, and you won't look back with regret.

Elementary, Middle, and High School Years

Parents of innovator children may instinctively know that they need to let their children learn how to manage their behaviors and homework, but often they just can't stand to see them fail. So instead they hover over them, reminding them, checking on them, criticizing, and sometimes punishing them for failing to perform according to the parents' expectations. At a young age, the innovator children can feel angry and resentful toward their intrusive, controlling parents. They want to be left alone, although they also may feel dependent and helpless at the same time. Every parent goes through this to some extent, but innovator parents with children face more challenges because their children are likely to experience a number of school-related issues. This is where many of the arguments that put great strain on the parent-child relationship begin. This is also the time and place where the mother and father of a rapid-fire thinker can begin to leverage their children's inherent abilities to be good problem solvers. It can be an opportunity to develop a culture of brainstorming, negotiating, and using reason and logic in the home as a response to their children's inabilities to get their homework done on time and stay off of the Internet and other electronic devices. Difficulties at school can become opportunities for children to get to know and understand themselves better and learn good problem-solving skills to address school issues and avoid taking things personally.

The following is one model for how parents involve the family in brainstorming, supporting, and helping their children find solutions. In traditional brainstorming sessions, simple techniques like timed responses are used to help people come up with new ideas.

Audrey's Story

Audrey is fifteen years old and having a hard time in English. She doesn't want to do the reading required of her assignments, and her compositions show that desire. Her pieces tend to be short and unorganized, and she often turns them in late. To help Audrey, the family decides to call a brainstorming meeting. One person is responsible for writing ideas on the board. Each person gets twenty seconds to come up with a solution before they move on to the next person. Using a timer to stay on track, Audrey's family came up with these solutions:

I. Audrey can video record herself reading the story out loud.

II. Audrey can create an outline and then ask an adult to help her evaluate it for organization.

III. For every two quality paragraphs Audrey writes, she can reward herself with fifteen jumps on the trampoline, dancing to a song, or five minutes of playing with the dog.

IV. When the paper is finished, Audrey can record herself reading it and play it for her family or a study buddy for feedback.

V. When Audrey has completed her paper and turned it in, she can have a pizza night where she orders the food, drinks, and desserts.

The important thing about brainstorming is that there are no wrong answers. Unusual and creative solutions are par for the course. In this process your children can learn they're good at problem solving, and more importantly, they can learn that they have valuable and important voices in the family. A good how-to book on brainstorming is *Brainstorm: The stories of Twenty American Kid Inventors* by Tom Tucker.

Childhood Peer Groups v. One-on-One Coaching

Elementary School

Peer groups for younger children with social anxiety and issues making friends can be run by school guidance counselors, therapists, and other children's support groups. In these groups children work on social interactions with other children who have trouble making or keeping friends. From my previous work in schools, I learned that when kids are invited to come to a special group because they have been specially selected for their attributes instead of their disabilities, they are proud to be included.

Sometimes younger children may need child therapists or "worry doctors" to help them figure things out. Often with young children, an intervention can involve a combination of family and school personnel, therapists, and doctors. It can take the village to help the children.

Middle School

Middle school students can respond especially well to groups. When presented as a privilege instead of a stigma, these groups can enhance self-esteem. I once had a classroom of gifted students with ADHD who were all in middle school. Since we were a separate class, other kids would pick on my students, make fun of them, and call them names. When we began doing smart and fun things like science fairs, plays, and art shows in front of the whole school during Friday assemblies, we stood out because we were the only class doing such things. Soon we were looked upon as the smart, capable, and gifted class. Then the abuse stopped, and students began begging to join our group.

High School

One-on-one coaching can be the best way to support innovators through their adolescent years. But sometimes parents cannot afford the cost. If, as a mother or father, you don't have the money to pay for coaching services, you may want to try talking to your school about creating a peer group for kids with the innovator brain type. If this cannot be done through your child's school, you can reach out to your community and other ADHD patents whose children have the same issues. Creating a support group for parents and one for teens at the same time is an even better idea since both patents and adolescent children will require a different kind of support. CHADD (Children and Adults with ADHD) provides a structure for doing this via satellite groups across the country. CHADD is a great place to share stories with other parents and ADHD professionals, find out about good resources, and learn what works when it comes to strategies to help your child through these difficult years.

Additional Ways to Create Peer Groups

Some parents have been successful at approaching the special education folks in the school to find out if there is an ADD/ADHD group that would be right for their children, and if not, they sometimes ask how the school would feel if they started one. You will probably want to get other parents of children labeled with ADD, ADHD, or Asperger's syndrome to join you in making the request. A group of concerned parents who won't take no for an answer can be a persuasive force for getting things done. Teachers can also be good advocates for starting such groups, although typically they do not have the influence that an organized group of parents have.

You may also be able to write a proposal and get grants or seed money from a pharmaceutical company that may be looking for a way to help the larger ADHD community. Find a community that already has an existing ADHD peer group and learn from them how to go about setting one up and what you will need to make it successful. I have found that well-informed parents may also be interested in supporting such groups even if their children do not have ADD because they realize that a rising tide lifts all boats. And don't forget to publicize your venture so you don't leave out anyone who could be important to your cause.

Jerry's Story

I have many students in my coaching practice who do quite well at alleviating their symptoms and challenges when they stay on course and won't give up. One of my students named Jerry came to coaching because he was a smart kid who did fine in school up until the ninth grade when he entered high school. He began to struggle soon after that. He did well in the few subjects that interested him but poorly in subjects considered more important like math and science, topics he did not like. Jerry was failing these subjects now. His parents were very concerned, and he was starting to give up. No one understood what the issue was.

This is one of my favorite stories, and it happened early on in my coaching career. It's the story of how Jerry was able to overcome what no one believed he could overcome and achieve what no one believed he could achieve. But before I begin, I want to give you a hint of things to come in Jerry's story.

Jerry just wouldn't give up. He would quit over and over again, but he never gave up. That is key if you want to have a life you're proud of, and at the tender ages of thirteen, fourteen, fifteen, and sixteen, Jerry learned what many adults never learn. If you don't give up, you get there.

Jerry was an African-American kid who lived in a neighborhood where there were both good and bad role models. Unfortunately for him and due to the challenges he had with managing his own behavior, he tended to make friends with the kids who either didn't do well in school or didn't want to go to school. He wasn't getting his homework done or paying attention in class. As a result, he was not getting along with his parents. Jerry was struggling in his urban school system, where he was able to lose himself in the crowd. He tried hard not to stand out and draw attention to himself. His confidence had become so eroded that he was ready to fade permanently into the background. His family had tried everything to help him, but nothing seemed to work. In middle school Jerry fell far behind in his schoolwork and began talking about quitting school. Then in the eighth grade, Jerry's family discovered ADHD coaching and decided to try it in the hope that Jerry's education could be saved.

Jerry's path was a constant struggle. For every good step forward, there seemed to be three steps backward. Jerry could not organize his work. He didn't write down his assignments or understand how to do them. He wasted time surfing on his computer and playing video games. Every night he put off doing his homework until it was too late, and studying was beyond his capability. In elementary school Jerry had succeeded in scraping by through the extra attention teachers and parents had given him and the one-on-one help disability classes provided. When he reached middle school, the services and extra attention he was used to getting was not as available. More importantly, the extra help that he had gotten earlier in his schooling that was intended to teach him how to work independently by the time he got to middle school had not succeeded. The plan had backfired, and Jerry was the unintended victim.

The first step with Jerry was to bolster his confidence by helping him see that he could learn how to succeed in school if he got the help he really needed and to teach him that having an innovator brain did not make him stupid, just different. Helping Jerry explore his strengths and talents started a process of opening his mind to a potential new and empowering interpretation of himself. Since Jerry was convinced he was a loser when it came to school, this was no easy task. Along with the necessity of building confidence and improving Jerry's outlook on the future, there was the immediate need for him to get organized, get his homework done, and pay attention in class. The first few months were devoted to helping him understand the specific behaviors that were not working for him and learn why they weren't working. We explained to him that he was able to learn the behaviors that would help him better meet expectations at school. He could set up a program where he would begin to take strong steps toward independent functioning.

At the start Jerry constantly fell off track. He was stubborn and refused to change. He would succeed at getting a good grade on a paper or achieve a superior test score, and then at the next opportunity, he would revert back to his old and less successful habits and would fail again. This often caused Jerry to feel overwhelmed, falling back into fears of inability and inadequacy and giving up. He blamed his teachers for his issues because they either couldn't teach or had taken a dislike to him. He was afraid to ask for help because he would look stupid, and he would constantly forget to make sure he understood how to do his homework before he left school. He continued to believe that his classmates and everyone around him were smarter and better than he was, and to handle such an insult to his ego and psyche, he withdrew.

Jerry struggled to maintain consistent improvement in the wake of so much going wrong. To counteract his difficulties, the plan for Jerry was to ensure that he improved in small increments that were substantial enough to keep his confidence up and make sure he did not give up on himself.

By the time Jerry had arrived at his junior year in high school four years later, he was completing most of his homework and was no longer getting grades below a C. He had more confidence in himself as judged by his willingness to ask for help from his teachers, tutors, and after-school aides. He had a girlfriend and no longer felt like an outcast.

He felt confident enough to apply to college and even include a top-rate school that was the first on his wish list. In spite of the many challenges of college applications, SATs, and emotional ups and downs, Jerry managed to achieve a 3.0 or B average—the best he had ever achieved in school.

I think it's safe to say that in spite of all his progress, the final chapter in Jerry's story surprised everyone. After he interviewed and visited all of the colleges on his list, Jerry was selected to attend his number-one school, a very prestigious college that few were able to get into. That college was likely able to see the good in Jerry and what he had overcome to get to where he was. They made a good call. Jerry has been there for two years so far, and he continues to compete successfully with his classmates and make outstanding progress.

Most people did not expect Jerry to achieve so much. When people heard about the college he had been accepted to, they were amazed. The lesson for all of us might be to never underestimate the power of someone with the innovative brain to persist and succeed no matter how impossible the odds of making it may seem. Jerry would certainly qualify as the poster child for achieving success. He had the faith to keep going against what often seemed like a battle against insurmountable odds.

When Should Children Begin Coaching?

Innovator children are ready for coaching between the ages of twelve and fourteen when they have the understanding and motivation to learn new behavior strategies and take responsibility for their actions. Some reasons to hire coaches for teenagers include the following:

- How much better would a coach be than an upset parent who is consistently nagging them?

- Taking into account getting good grades, achieving excellent test scores, completing projects, and getting homework done, how are they doing?
- How are they getting along with their teachers and classmates?
- How confident are they when it comes to fulfilling expectations—both theirs and those of their teachers and parents?
- How comfortable are they in social situations?
- Do they worry and feel anxious more than what is normally expected for someone their ages, and is it keeping them up at night?
- How forgetful are they, and what effect does that have on their grades and relationships?
- Are their backpacks cluttered and messy, and are their papers, notebooks, and binders disorganized?
- Do they procrastinate with starting their homework, studying for tests, and beginning projects?
- Are they prone to staying awake at night to either complete schoolwork or research on the computer?

Drugs and Sex

I didn't outright forbid drugs and sex with my own children when they were teens, and I wasn't totally laissez-faire either. Being a child of the 60s and 70s, I had a lot of soul searching to do regarding what I had done myself versus what I wanted for my children. I knew I wanted to be aware of their comings and goings and to keep the lines of communication open. This meant I wouldn't take a hard stand on important issues. I encouraged communication and discussion instead of just forbidding them to do something they really wanted to do. With these intentions in mind, I tried to do my best. I must admit that at times I stumbled along, praying for a good outcome. But I was involved in knowing who they were as they grew and what they were doing to the best of my ability when they were not with me. Looking back now, this approach worked the best during the times when I included my kids in the decision-making process, whether it was a decision that affected them only or a decision that affected the whole family. I think that the basics like being honest and spending as much time with our children as possible can't be overemphasized. The feedback I have gotten from my son and daughter confirms that. In retrospect, they say it was more important that I was guiding them and setting limitations, although they said they hated it at the time.

I know my kids did things I did not approve of. After all, they were teenagers, and I could not be around them all of the time. On occasion, my son would sneak out of the house in the middle of the night and drive around with his friends long before he had a driver's license. When my daughter was fourteen, there were times when she would lie about where she was going and what she was doing. At the age of eighteen, she apologized for acting that way. These things happened. I also knew my son and daughter's friends and who their parents were, and I paid attention to changes in my kids' behavior.

When parents don't know how to respond to their innovator children's behavior, conflict and chaos can dominate. Help your children come up with solutions to their own behavior and offer them choices. Encourage them and talk them through failures. Get help with caring for your children. Talk to mental health professionals, avoid labeling, and be patient with their progress. Understanding and behavior changes take time.

Teen peers who are friends with those who have innovator brains often describe their friends' behaviors as impulsive, annoying, flakey, aggravating, incompetent, unreliable, flirty, tactless, eccentric, or immature. Add to that impression the fact that preteens and teens are at an emotionally vulnerable stage. They feel better if they're putting someone else down, and they tend to put down those who are different. We must also be aware of the dividing line between behavior that is meant to provoke and behavior that turns into serious bullying—an issue our country is finally paying attention to.

Not all rapid-fire thinkers have serious peer group issues. How they interact with their peers can depend upon a supportive home environment, how well he or she fits in at school, and which of the so-called annoying traits listed previously they may have. For me, my low self-esteem came from my family more than it came from my peers.

If only kids labeled with ADD and ADHD could understand that their rapid-fire thinking abilities matched with their creative talents and problem-solving capacities actually makes them leaders rather than victims!

The nature of a group is to pull everyone into sameness. By nature, groups sustain mediocrity. If you want to be exceptional, eventually you're going to have to step away from the group. It is important to understand and to absorb this principle before the age of thirteen. If not, it usually won't take root in the mind until after the age of twenty. Teenagers are not usually open to this message because belonging is of the utmost importance in adolescence. They tend to believe that their peer groups know better than they do. It is our job to be there when they are ready to talk to us, ask us questions, and open up. They will need to hear this message: "Question the group. Don't follow it."

Here are some perpetually negative peer messages:

- "You don't fit in."
- "We don't really like you."
- "You're weird and stupid."
- "No one gets you."
- "You're fat, ugly, flat-chested, and/or dumb."
- "You don't know how to act."

When innovators are twelve or thirteen, it's good for them to understand how the teenage dynamic works.

Kids who grow up hearing, "What is wrong with you? Don't you ever pay attention? You never learn," a hundred times more every day than the average child figures out that there must be something wrong with them. It's not complicated to children. At a time when it is most important to lay the foundation for a life of success with self-love and love for others, many rapid-fire thinkers are laying down layer upon layer of self-hatred and frustration.

One of the problems is that they can't see themselves in a true light. They are looking at themselves according to how many times they mess up compared to other people. They see rejection in other people's behavior whether it is there or not. Rapid-fire thinkers need a translator. They need someone who really sees what is going on and can articulate it for them.

As a rapid-fire thinker, I will tell you straight that being a kid who is a rapid-fire thinker and who does not have the tools to channel and harvest that wonderful energy can be an awful way to live. Any minute you might open up your mouth, and something stupid will come out. While everyone in class is trying to learn algebra, you're thinking about what's going to happen in your next class because you aren't prepared. Besides, this class is so boring. While other students are fixing their attentions on the teacher, you space out because you're so tired from trying, trying, and trying to focus or because you seldom get enough sleep. Unfortunately the result of all this unharnessed and misunderstood energy can be equal amounts of anxiety and depression.

As stated earlier, in order to help their children, parents must first help themselves by getting help with their own personal problems. We all have the need to routinely observe ourselves. We need to keep learning and growing and getting feedback on how we're doing. We need this for ourselves and for our children. When we know how to keep ourselves from becoming stressed out, our children will be able to learn that too. When we treat one another and even strangers with respect, we're giving our children a leg up on leading a life of purpose and integrity and believing they can do so too. When we take responsibility for our own lives and for the things we're proud of, our children will ultimately learn to create the outcomes and lives they truly want.

How to Help Your Innovator Friends, Family, and Coworkers

It will be challenging.

It takes time to learn to pause, take a deep breath, and learn how to respond. Medicine helps. Meditation helps. Anything that calms the brain but doesn't numb us out or take us away from reality (e.g., substance abuse) helps. Having a third party reflect back to us what they see enables us to create new communication patterns so we can turn the corner from unsatisfying relationships to satisfying ones. That is what good coaches do every day for individuals and couples. But what about the rest of us? How can we help friends, coworkers, or members of our own family with innovator brains in a way that works for us and for them?

They don't think they need help. They don't want to get help. Calling a coach and setting up an appointment feels like being pinned to the wall as a failure for many people. They may mask this by justifying reasons for waiting. I often encounter people who are desperate for help. They've come so far that they've made a phone call. Then they back down and decide they can't afford to work with a coach. A few years later, they realize that they could have had different lives if they'd had the courage to invest in changing undesirable behaviors into powerful new ones.

I often tell people that the quality of their lives for the rest of their lives could be worth the money they would pay someone to help them change what needs changing and improve what needs improving. People with ADHD are known for not seeing themselves as clearly as others see them. Complicating matters, of course, is that they often come for help with anxiety disorders, depression, bipolar disorder, OCD, or addictions.

Your beautiful baby boy is now fifteen, and as soon as you see him in the morning, you get a pain in your gut. Your interactions with him have disintegrated into you drilling him on tasks to be completed while he refuses to make eye contact and pretends to ignore you. Then he blurts out something rude and stomps out. That may happen pretty much every morning like clockwork. When this happens, remember that you can and should find the right help for you and your son and that you have the strength, patience, and resilience to make the right choices and decisions as a parent.

Parents can be advocates both at home and in their children's school.

I was once an activist teacher. I preferred bringing parents into the fold and teaching them how to be advocates for their children.

In the 60s and 70s, I became deeply and completely committed to civil rights, feminism, and the antiwar movement. This is where I learned how to work cooperatively and successfully with others who also believed strongly in what I believed in. In the trenches I learned to advocate, persist, and not give up. We didn't know we couldn't change the world, but we learned how to make a difference and change minds. We learned how to get things done.

I brought this sense of standing up for what is right and fighting the good fight into my teaching. Actually I preferred to work with the "unwanted" problem students. I thought they needed someone to speak for them, and I also thought we needed to give them a chance. So for the next 17 years I either taught in or ran programs for Boston's most challenging students-the ones who threw chairs across the room, abused drugs in the classroom closets, and hung one another out fourth-story windows. It really was like going into combat every day, and I dressed the part. What drew me to this work was that these kids had never thought of themselves as anything other than losers. The more I cared for them and believed in them, the more they fought me in their attempts to prove I would give up on them like everyone else had. What I learned from that experience was that you can turn kids (people) around if you are consistent in your approach and you are sincere in your feelings. Even kids with a history of dysfunction and despair can learn to trust.

Certainly parents are capable of becoming activists for the sake of their children. If you need to, you can. No matter how stressed, busy, or financially challenged you are, if you need to find support for your child, then there are ways to do it. Not only through the normal academic support channels but also when you start to rustle the bushes, you often find other parents eager to join you in setting up support groups and getting the right services for their children.

PART 4

The Stigma-Free Innovator Life

The final portion of this book synthesizes all of the preceding lessons so that we can look forward to a future, one that is defined by the ability of the innovator brain, not the limitations of a disability label. This last part of this guide has the proven strategies, the right mindset, and the crucial understandings that are necessary to ensure the unique gifts and inventive ability of this brain type can be shared with the outside world. As a result of being your own advocate through finding and declaring your purpose, visualizing your success, and creating a blueprint for your future you will be prepared to step forward with confidence in yourself and your destiny.

CHAPTER 13

Becoming Your Own Advocate

Over and over again, Innovators find themselves caught in situations where they feel misunderstood and unjustly blamed. This emotional re-action, if not changed to taking-action, will keep innovators stuck in a place of powerlessness. All too often, instead of taking the bull by the horns, innovators back down from advocating for themselves because they feel guilty as charged.

Applying negative interpretations to our behavior makes that negative opinion of ourselves stronger. Having a negative opinion of ourselves reinforces the opportunity for other people to pick up on that energy and create their own negative impressions of us. Why not decide to focus on the positive and uplifting result you truly want to have in your life? Unlike Debbie Downer from *Saturday Night Live*, *you* can wake up to your negative perspective of yourself and choose to behave differently. You can become willing to get help from a professional ADHD coach with the goal of creating a positive mind-set. With help, you can create your own positive results in your life and become a sought-after communicator. It always comes back to achieving the right mind-set and attitude.

The Source of Conflicts

If you are a rapid-fire thinker, you can put your inclination to be argumentative and make your point to good use. When you harness your natural desire to rebel against the status quo with the intention to create a better outcome, you can form mutually beneficial relationships. Let's see how it's done.

Successfully Handling Conflict with Others

When we were growing up, many of us were discouraged from expressing anything that went against the program laid out by parents, schools, and society at large. We reacted by stuffing our feelings deep down inside of us. As a consequence, we became alienated from our true feelings and thoughts in order to fit in with the larger group. This is where we first experienced the worst kind of conflict, not being allowed to be ourselves.

I can embrace conflict now because the fear of it doesn't control me any longer. Here is an affirmation for you to try: "I believe in the powerful wisdom and self-loving thoughts of my soul and spirit that free me to live the life that is right for me." I have a routine of recognizing my negative thoughts, subtracting them, and embedding positive affirmations into my new consciousness.

Triggers are important when it comes to managing challenges because they keep us from seeing what is truly going on in the moment. A trigger takes us back to a previous time when something went wrong and a painful memory gets activated. For example, two years ago I had an embarrassing experience when I was presenting a project in front of a group of important people. I botched the order of things, completely lost my focus, and did not deliver what I thought was a coherent presentation. For the next couple of times I presented, I was taken back to that moment when I was overcome with fear and unable to function. I knew that fear had nothing to do with what was going on right then, but the similarity to what happened before tricked me into falling back into those same feelings of embarrassment.

A trigger is a circumstance that recreates the feelings and behaviors from another traumatic time. If rapid-fire thinkers have encountered conflict on a continual basis, chances are they have a few triggers stored up in their subconscious. The key to getting control over triggers is to watch for them. The more you are able to identify and observe your triggers, the less you will fall into their traps.

Here is something you can practice. Pay attention to the feeling you get in the pit of your stomach when a bad or painful memory is triggered. Notice the memory that you recall by the trigger. Write it down. Every day for the next week, you are going to see how often that particular memory gets triggered for you. When you have it, you are going to forgive yourself and whoever—or whatever—was involved in that memory and kiss it good-bye. You are going to continue to do that practice until the memory no longer holds the charge that caused the trigger in the first place.

A good friend of mine grew up with two parents who used demeaning words and loud voices to control and bully people around them. Whenever she sits down in a formal group and people begin to speak, she gets knots in her stomach, afraid that they will launch into an endless, pointless speech, argument, or public reprimand. Because that memory triggers her, she avoids being part of events, meetings, or get-togethers where people "have the floor."

Another example I often hear about is the following: It is 4:00 p.m. on Saturday. This is the time that you have agreed to call your mother. At 3:30 p.m., your mind is triggered, and you begin to feel angry feelings. Your negative thoughts create chaos inside of you. You really don't want to talk to your mother. So what is it about your mother that you need to express? Where are you holding back being truthful with her? (You can interchange mother with husband, boss, brother, sister, dad, etc.)

Most of our sense of victimization actually results from not fully expressing ourselves. I have discovered that much of the time, misunderstandings with others result from not telling them everything – the whole story - including sharing our feelings. Think back to how this applies to your own experience. Remember how many times conflicts with others were cleared up through clarifying the whole and complete truth, including the feelings that made you feel vulnerable or afraid.

Three things can happen simultaneously when you tell the truth. First of all, you step out of victim mode and into self-protection/self-love mode. Secondly you have treated the other people with respect by believing that they can treat you with respect. Finally you have silenced your triggered impulse.

Never give up and give into your triggered emotions and negative thinking. Fight back! You may go down a few times. We all do. And you may find yourself swimming in anger and self-pity. Just get up again and keep trying. Always ask for help if you need it. Remember that if you keep going and do not give up, you will learn to conquer fear and negativity and come out on top. That's the way it works.

Everyone can be afraid of conflict under certain circumstances. You're in your boss's office. You say to yourself, "If I argue with my boss, I will do myself harm." Other common thoughts regarding conflict include: *People will leave me. They won't like me. A good family has peace and not conflict.*

Not knowing how to engage in conflict paralyzes us and causes us to go through life on crutches, never free from the conflict within. A way out of this dilemma is to find resolution through asking yourself, "Am I being honest with myself and with other people?"

I grew up learning how to be dishonest—dishonest with myself and with others about how I felt and what I wanted. I didn't realize at the time that I was living half a life. By always stuffing deep inside of me who I was and how I felt, I was unconsciously marginalizing myself. When I was seventeen, I left my family and began the process of finding my voice again. I discovered the sweetness, freedom, and power of being honest with myself and other people.

Healing begins with compassion for the people who hurt us. That compassion is followed by forgiveness. Before we are able to communicate a good self-image with healthy boundaries, we must experience this inner healing. In the case of forgiving my older sister and my mother, I had to sit down and try to see things from their points of view and imagine the unfulfilled needs of their own that contributed to the people they became. When parents treat children harshly, it is very likely that was how they were treated. Sometimes hurtful behaviors and mental illnesses can get passed on to the next generation. We must all help one another so that doesn't happen to the children who are coming along.

Compassion has helped me find forgiveness. And practicing forgiveness has helped me build greater self-esteem.

Not all relationships require such a deep level of healing. Sometimes setting boundaries is just realizing that we are being dishonest and deciding to tell the truth. The truth really can—and often does—set us free.

Effective Practices For Innovators

1. Ask Permission

One thing all rapid-fire thinkers profit from is a collaborative approach. This goes for both innovators and those with whom they interact. Instead of criticizing or confronting an innovator, ask: "Can I share observations with you? Would you like some help? What if we tried doing this another way?"

2. Learn from Mistakes

We all must come to terms with being wrong. Making mistakes is how we learn and grow. No mistakes – no growth and not much of a life. Don't take it personally when you screw up. Highly successful people say that being willing to make mistakes was the reason they got so far in life. Didn't Babe Ruth also hold the record for number of strike- outs? Our tendency is to magnify our own mistakes and failures while being blind to the mistakes and failures of others. While we can't always see people making mistakes, like us they too are often in error. Yet we are quick to forgive the failures of others but unwilling to forgive our own. Starting now you can do something about this. Celebrate the great learning and wisdom that comes from being wrong and use it to rise above the others who let the fear of making mistakes hold them back.

3. Build Self-Worth

I have a client named Patricia with an anxiety disorder, and she has a fear that people don't like her. She worries she'll be rejected because she makes a fool of herself no matter how hard she tries to act normal. Patricia avoids having real conversations and building relationships because she's afraid of rejection.

Most of my painful memories involve people coming down on me and not sticking up for myself when I had the chance. Because I didn't have the habit of advocating for myself, I didn't see what was right in front of my nose, specifically an honest look at what was really going on. Over time I had been conditioning myself to accept the pain of being abandoned by those around me. Building my own self-esteem became my most important goal in life. Although it took much time and effort, I was eventually able to move from feeling abandoned to feeling like I mattered. I did this with the help of the next practice.

4. Focus on Strengths, Not Weaknesses

It is important to become clear and convinced about the strengths and talents that are unique to you. They are your gifts and secrets to your success. They are what you will learn to use to your advantage in order to overcome and compensate for any deficiencies like inattention, impulsivity, and disorganization. When you find and fully embrace them, you will discover that you are exceptionally capable and competent in your true gifts in this lifetime. What do you love to do? What is important to you? What are you good at? What do you dream about or long for? Those are clues about what you are likely to be successful at and enjoy doing. But you must be careful not to become confused. Being happy with a particular vocation is not always supported by the society around you, your friends, your family, or financial compensation. You must be strong in your commitment to your own life and happiness. If you go by the advice and perspective of others, you will more than likely never be happy.

Get someone to help you find your strengths and then write them down. Next design a plan that includes the monthly, weekly, and daily actions and steps you will need to take to utilize your strengths and achieve your goals.

Background to Being Ready to Create Your Life Purpose

To begin the process of retraining your mind, you have to believe that you can succeed. Many rapid-fire thinkers I meet talk about their brains as separate mechanisms. "It's just something up there that controls me, and I don't have a say in it." So the first step in taking over the reins of your thoughts is to believe that you can control your brain. There is a power within you, and that is the power of your authentic will, which is far greater than that of your body or mind. Often referred to as "willpower," this creative power within you wants to speak for you, but it can only be that spokesperson if you listen to it. You can listen to it by paying attention and acting on that first idea you get. That initial idea is the voice of your true will, and your true will knows what you desire and what is truly possible for you. The voice that comes next, the second voice, is the one that immediately tells you it's a bad idea and you cannot succeed. This second voice is your inauthentic voice or the naysaying saboteur. It is the voice of fear. You will need to work to identify both of these voices so that you can understand how they operate in your everyday life and how the latter keeps you stuck in unhappy, unfulfilling patterns of behavior. Once you understand how that happens, you can gain more control over your thinking and choose empowering thoughts over disempowering ones. You can choose the voice of your true will over your saboteur. Believe that this power is in you and hold on to it as your main tool against uncontrolled impulses.

Then you can begin to listen for the negative thinking patterns running around in your brain. Hear them inside yourself and how they occur within you. The ability to listen to your own thoughts is one of the primary things that separate humans from animals. Animals do not think about how they are thinking.

Start responding to your thoughts with these questions: "How do I feel when I think that thought? What happens as a result of that thought? What am I willing to do to change this negative thinking pattern? What help do I need to seek out in order to change this problematic thinking pattern? What will be possible for me after I have changed this negative thinking pattern?"

Write your answers down. What do you notice?

These thoughts determine what you have and don't have in your life. Thinking is driving the results in your life. Some typical negative thought patterns follow this structure: *Things never work out for me in romantic relationships.* This thought makes sure that you cut off new relationship opportunities. Notice how whenever you think about having a relationship, you get that feeling of fear in your stomach. We avoid what we fear.

Here is another common negative thought: *I don't know how to get out of poverty/debt. I'll never have the money I need and want.* This thought seals the contract on your inability to make and accumulate money. So you can say instead, "I have all the money I need and want," and if you keep saying it over and over again day after day and week after week, you will sooner or later attract that result into your life. Here are some of my favorite quotes: "What we believe becomes the very substance of our cells" (Chasing Deer from *American Indian Prophecies*). "We become what we repeatedly do (think)" (Aristotle). "You are what you think about all day long" (Dr. Robert Schuller). "If you think you can or you think you can't—you're right" (Henry Ford).

Most of us are not aware of how our subconscious minds are telling us what to do. We wake up in the morning, and by the time we're driving to work, we've said to ourselves thirty times, "My boss is a jerk," or we've asked, "What's wrong with me?"

Look for the source within yourself rather than blaming the world. We are the source of all of our actions and results. After we believe that we can control our thoughts and become aware of what we are thinking, we can then start to allow opportunities to come in. Life really opens up when you turn on your "receive" mode instead of your "out of order" mode. Instead of mentally living in a corner with light shining through a crack, light pours in on all sides. Instead of saying, "Maybe, maybe not," life becomes one big "Yes, I will!"

"Yes, I can have a life that is joyful, happy, and resonates with my deepest desires" is a great affirmation. When rapid-fire thinkers do this work, they are more likely to find innovator brain issues in their lives easier to change. Why? They are motivated by joy rather than stopped by pain.

The road to finding my purpose in life began by sitting down every night on the side of the bed and obsessively planning the next day. I put all my energies into creating ways of staying on track. I know that if I didn't start there, the rest would be hopeless. I just had to get my rapid-firing brain under control. Here were my rules at the time in my life when I was working hard to get on track:

- Rule 1: Plan the week ahead.
- Rule 2: Check my plan the night before.
- Rule 3: Carry my planner everywhere I go.
- Rule 4: Remember to carry my planner everywhere I go.

- Rule 5: Put notes all over the house to remember to carry my planner everywhere I go. (I wanted to nail my planner to my side because I knew I'd forget where I left it.)

Experience taught me that in order to change and grow, I had to allow myself to make mistakes—sometimes over and over again—or I'd never get there. When I didn't plan ahead, I suffered. When I forgot to write something down, I suffered. When I didn't get the answers I needed, I suffered. So I got better at planning. I learned how to schedule appointments and use the time in between to complete tasks. I learned to put sticky notes everywhere. I organized my office constantly, constantly, constantly, and never went to bed without everything put away and ready for the next day. It took a few years before I felt I would survive the whole thing, but in the process I realized I had learned a lot about how to manage myself. It was definitely worth it, even though in the beginning it occupied a lot of my time. Now it's second nature, and I don't notice spending a lot of time on scheduling or task management like I did at the beginning. That is what happens when you meet a need. It disappears from your to-do list.

When I found myself in the process of becoming an ADHD coach, I wanted to be able to show my clients what could be done with techniques and support systems in addition to the medication they were taking. I felt it was important that people with ADHD see that there were other ways to harness their ADHD gifts successfully with or without medication. They needed to see the possibility that in addition to medications, coaching and therapy could be very effective tools of change.

I took various combinations of drugs before I found the one that worked for me. I hate to take anything, even Tylenol. It took me a long time to learn to take the supplements and the medications necessary to maintaining my health. It turns out that was just my drama. Medication made a big difference in my life. I took it regularly until I got control over my behavior through coaching, a lot of hard work, and practice, practice, practice. Then I found I didn't need it anymore.

The following are the most important habits and behaviors I have found to live and work in ways that allow me, someone with an innovator brain, to use my extraordinary talents and abilities to my advantage:

- I learned what I can and what I cannot do without certain structures in place.
- I can share my limitations with confidence, knowing I am training the people around me to give me the exact support I will need to succeed. Here are some examples: "I need firm deadlines to get the project and deliverables in on time." "Daily reminders help me stay focused on achieving my goals." "I will need to see the big picture to understand the details." "I will want to collaborate on designing the steps and coming up with a time frame for getting them done."
- I will be completely aware of what my strengths are. I will use them to help manage my weaknesses. When I know I can come up with a first-class solution in record time, I am a very valuable person to myself, my family and friends, and my place of employment.
- I plan the week ahead and anticipate the time frames needed for everything by doubling the amount of time I think I need.
- Before I plan my week, I prioritize my tasks according to my career goals and the vision I have for my life.
- I line up in advance the people and other resources I may need to achieve my goals. I'm careful not to run the risk of floundering and falling off track, chasing shiny balls, and playing the role of a stimulation-seeking missile.
- I remember I will always need to adhere to these rules and use them to replace the motivation my brain naturally lacks.

- I focus and concentrate on doing my work in the least distracting environment possible. I avoid stimulating activities associated with the computer, television, phone, video games, and similar ways of procrastinating. Having music and background noise, however, can help me focus and concentrate if the lyrics aren't distracting.

Until we embrace our personal challenges and limitations, we will continue to be a hostage to our feelings of deficiency, and we will be subject to self-condemning emotions. When we embrace our emotions, we are able to fly above the forces that can hold us down. When we are able to be fully present to our talents and gifts and accept our own limitations, we can defy obstacles and flourish in spite of them. Remember that innovators have the power, intelligence, and creativity to change anything that gets in their way.

Because the innovator brain prefers the present moment to the past or the future, this way of thinking is ideally suitable for finding a cure to cancer. This is because the rapid-fire thinking trait so typical of this brain type is ideal for coming up with solutions and inventions quickly and accurately. However, when people need to manage their everyday affairs, plan ahead, stick to a schedule, and complete projects on time, this can be a less than helpful type of brain. In your life you will learn how to keep using the best of your innovator brain and still maintain the critical strategies and behaviors for planning ahead and sticking to a consistent routine.

When we foster our connection with spirit through intention, focus, and stillness, we can rise from a barren desert like a phoenix and realize a life of purpose and fulfillment.

When you gain control over your behavior, you can learn self-support structures, develop routines to keep you on track, and build a network of helpful people around you. You may always have the need to inhibit behavior, but eventually you learn to seek the stimulation you need at the right times and in the right ways.

While we can all be proud to have the type of brain that can invent, create, and solve problems, we also need to use our strengths to learn to manage the kind of behavior that makes us disorganized and inattentive, causing other people to bark disapproval at us on a regular basis.

CHAPTER 14

Declaring Your Purpose

When we consider creative ideas and innovative thinking as major strengths of this brain type, we may want to ask how we can make the most of this strength. Spokespeople for both our own economy and the global economy are claiming that innovation is even more in demand as we compete on the world stage in the fields of economics, technology, and engineering. People in these fields where innovative solutions are the key to success are most often those with the innovator brain type. That is as it should be.

However, these numbers remain low when compared to the wealth of innovators out there who have the same skills but do not have either the understanding or the confidence to make the most of their innovative gifts. Too many people are slipping through the cracks, leading lackluster and difficult lives as a result of having been labeled ADHD. Feeling incompetent and fearing failure prevent potential star innovators from competing for positions in industries where out-of-the-box ideas and thinking are sorely needed.

This is a shame and something we need to address as soon as possible. So what do we need to do about it? Where do we start?

Let me share a story with you about a client of mine who will help highlight what the problems are and what we can do about them.

Josh's Story

Josh was a highly intelligent and capable achiever throughout school and college. Born with the innovator brain type, he was educated about his brain and given the tools to succeed at a young age. He felt supported by his parents and teachers throughout his early life. Diagnosed in elementary school, he received coaching, tutoring, and therapy throughout his school years to help him understand how to use his strengths to compensate for his weaknesses. Josh flourished as a result of the structure offered in his educational environments. He grew to depend on them.

When Josh got his first job, he was expecting to be just as successful as he had been in school. However, problems began to surface not long after he started. For the first few months Josh did well in his new position and quickly learned the rules. He got along well with his superiors and his coworkers. Expectations were high that he would do well and make the company proud to have him on board, and at first that is exactly what happened. But at his job there was no oversight of his progress. No one was checking to see if he understood what he was doing and if he was completing tasks correctly and on time. There were no clearly spelled out steps of how to communicate with teams and representatives from other departments. No one had been identified as his go-to person when he needed help, and so he did his best to carry on without it.

Josh was used to pleasing people because that is what he had always done in school. But at his job he often felt confused about what was being asked of him. He had trouble staying focused because of noise and distractions. He found it difficult to meet his deadlines and to pay attention during meetings. Josh became more and more confused and therefore more and more anxious and doubtful of his ability. He began to feel he was not on the same level as those around him, including the guy who had been hired at the same time as him. Worry and anxiety were building. He felt that he was not doing what was required of him and would soon be called out about it. He started to feel he was drowning, and he didn't know how to save himself. Then the moment he was dreading came. His boss called him into his office for a private meeting. Josh felt as if the ax was getting ready to fall.

Josh's boss wanted to know how Josh felt about his job and how things were going. Josh answered honestly, saying he was not sure but suspected he was not doing as well as he should be doing. His boss asked him if he had pursued help in the areas that were confusing to him, and Josh told him he didn't know who to go to. When the meeting concluded, Josh was assigned a mentor who would be there when he needed help with his stumbling blocks. However, there was no mention of Josh's need for structure and accountability because of his brain type.

The mentor was helpful but not helpful enough. Like Josh's boss, he did not understand what Josh really needed and complained that Josh was coming to him for help way too often. He suggested to Josh's boss that Josh might not be able to handle the job. After eight months, two negative performance reviews, and not much observable change on Josh's part, Josh was told he needed more help than the company was in a position to give him. They wished him the best, but unfortunately they had to let him go.

It took Josh a year and a half to get the help that would turn his situation around. It first Josh spent a lot of time in therapy working on his wounded ego and self-doubt. When he was not in therapy, he was in his bedroom. He had no social life and spent most of his time either in front of the computer or in front of the television. His parents anguished over what was going to become of him. They began to talk with Josh about other interventions, including in-patient care at a local psychiatric hospital.

Josh was not admitted to a hospital psychiatric unit. After eight months Josh began to snap out of it by realizing he didn't want to live in isolation any longer. He was tentative but willing to explore something new when he heard about ADHD coaching and decided to give it s try. Hesitant at first, Josh came to realize that I understood him in a way other people had not. He felt a great sense of relief when I told him that he was not permanently flawed and incapable of holding down a job. He was surprised to learn he may not be stupid or incompetent after all, but instead he lacked the right workplace skills.

Josh and I worked together for the next ten months. We focused on building his confidence. We worked on developing his understanding of the behaviors and workplace strategies he needed in order to be successful at work. Along the way he was able to develop a clear understanding of what had gone wrong previously. Josh was sad to learn that his biggest problem in his previous job was thinking he needed to overcome obstacles on his own. Had he not waited to get help the moment he needed it, he may not have dug such a deep hole, lost his footing, and found it impossible to get it back.

After about five months, Josh began to let go of the feeling that he had been sentenced to a life of being permanently flawed. He began to develop faith and hope in himself and the future. He was able to see how his educational environments had supported him in ways that the workplace could not, and for that reason, he had been unprepared for any job. He had not yet learned to be completely accountable to himself. Josh realized that always having had someone there to anticipate what he needed and when he needed it had hindered him from knowing how to get help on his own.

Most importantly, Josh and I worked on using his strengths and learning style to manage his daily and weekly tasks. Understanding how important routines are for people with ADHD, Josh developed a routine of taking time out on Sunday to plan the week ahead. But before he could do that, he needed an overall picture of the future broken into smaller and smaller increments.

Josh began the task of future planning by drawing a large pyramid with the top triangle representing his overarching goal for the year. Going from the top of the pyramid downward using horizontal lines drawn from one side to the other, he then broke his overarching goal into twelve monthly and fifty-two weekly goals. Now Josh was ready to tackle what he needed to do on a weekly basis to reach his twelve month overarching goal. His final step was to purchase a week by week planning book that allowed him to record in writing his tasks, appointments, projects, and items from his all important to do list. Josh liked how taking the time to do this much planning at the beginning made everything easier for him later on, especially because he was able to anticipate things coming up, stay focused, and avoid distractions. This didn't happen overnight. Josh had to work at it for a number of months to make this routine a consistent practice.

Keeping up with his tasks and priorities made him feel in control of his life and his accomplishments. It provided the motivation for Josh to keep going. It made it possible for him to feel better about himself and begin the process of forgiving his past. He began to remember what it was like to feel empowered in his life, something he had not felt since college. It was a gift to be able to watch Josh grab hold of his dreams and believe in them again.

Most importantly, Josh had developed the confidence to ask for help whenever he needed it. And soon he would be able to put what he had learned to the test. About a year and a half into our coaching relationship, Josh decided he was ready to look for a job in the financial industry, something he had wanted for a long time. He went on several interviews, but nothing seemed to be working in his favor. Still Josh remained hopeful. He kept at it month after month, letting his top three choices know on a regular basis he was still interested in working for them.

Josh eventually got a job at one of his three choices. A year into his new position, he called me to tell me that he had been seriously challenged since we had stopped working together but that he had good news for me. He reported that he had passed his performance review and had received a bonus! Clearly there was no stopping Josh now.

So what can we do to give more people like Josh the help they need so they can succeed? We need to provide help for children with this brain type in schools beginning in the first grade and continuing throughout high school and college. We also need to provide the public with an ongoing education so that people can understand what the innovator brain really is and how people with this brain type can be supported to function at their best.

How can all of us make the most of our creative strengths and help one another do the same? We can begin by advocating for ourselves and insisting on getting what we need to succeed in school, in our jobs, and in our personal lives. We can do our part to teach those around us what our creative innovator strengths really are and the structure, strategies, and routines we need to be successful. We can insist on believing in our own creative strengths and in our ability to make a unique contribution to the profession or career of our choice. And we can reach out to one another to ensure each of us gets the help we need so that we feel in control of all the domains of our lives.

As adults who have grown up hearing that we have attention deficit disorder, we need to literally deconstruct the false house of disorder where our self-esteem lives. In its place we need to build the castle of the gifted and talented.

As a rapid-fire thinker, you solve problems. From complex developmental problems when you were an infant to big world problems as an adult, you constantly evaluate, communicate, experiment, and fix problems. Your imagination never stops leaping over obstacles. Challenges that would frighten or stop many people are everyday apples and oranges for you. If someone says that it can't be done, you find a way to do it. If the issues are insurmountable and the damage unfixable, you can always build a bigger and better possibility.

People with the innovator gene are known for having an unlimited potential to create game-changing solutions and bring innovative ideas to life. You now have the opportunity to learn how you can use your ability to be innovative and bring extraordinary possibilities to your personal and professional life.

Finding Your Life's Purpose

In this chapter I will be talking about the importance of purpose. A life purpose comes from the soul or spirit, not from the conscious mind. It has to do with making a contribution to something outside of our own individual lives that matters to us. To figure it out, you have to connect to your soul and listen to it. You can sit around all day and use your logical, conscious brain to find your life purpose, but you won't come to an answer until you are willing to sit still, focus on a higher power, and listen to your wise inner voice. Meditation is one very effective way to do this. Having an ADHD or life coach who understands the process is another way. The combination of both is unbeatable.

There are a number of sages and coaches with their own unique ways of helping you uncover your life's purpose. Well-known quantum physicist Greg Mooers says, "Identity is living in alignment with what is most meaningful to us." In order to help us align with our true identities, he asks a series of questions that tie into our deepest beliefs and desires (Mooers Montana, 2015). Dr. Wayne Dyer calls on us to connect our intuition with our will or intention. "You must be what it is that you're seeking—that is, you need to put forth what you want to attract" (Dyer 2005)

Bridging Philosophy with Reality

As a society, we have been indoctrinated to listen to our conscious minds. Our conscious minds include everything that is a part of our awareness, including sensations, perceptions, memories, feelings, and fantasies triggered by the stimuli in our environment. Our unconscious mind is the keeper of the things hidden from our awareness, and as Freud believed, they "exert the greatest influence over us" (Freud, 1915). In relying only or mostly on our conscious mind, we miss out on the wisdom and answers available in our inner world from our authentic inner voices. In doing so, we allow one of our greatest assets to lay dormant. We have bought into the belief that we will find answers to our questions in materialism and technology. We've buried the idea of finding our own deeper truth as we skate along the surface of our lives, maintaining unsatisfying careers and disappointing relationships, making money at the expense of our well-being, collecting material possessions, ignoring the impact of our activities on the environment, and never asking the important questions, "Who am I, and why am I here?"

Our conscious mind also tends only to process thoughts and actions it sees as safe. Since our idea of safe comes from what we learned from any traumas or losses we experienced in the past, our conscious mind is actually running off of old fear-based scripts rather than on today's reality. This disconnect is especially painful to a rapid-fire thinker. Rapid–fire thinkers know what it feels like to solve a problem; however, when their conscious minds are running a loop between the present and the past, they are not getting anywhere. This leads to frustration and sometimes the need to hide behind addictions or other avoidance tactics.

It helps to know that we live in a world of two realities. The physical reality where we can touch, taste, and feel is not actually real when it comes to creating meaning in our lives. The reality where we develop meaning in our lives is our soul connection to the spiritual truth that resides inside and outside of us. When we base our lives on the material and on our physical senses, we find we tend to feel more empty than full.

Think of the people you know who are connected to their souls and spirits because they have made peace with their lives. They are satisfied with the truth about who they are and confident in the purpose they are devoted to. They are in full alignment with their soul purposes and in accordance with their spiritual sides. This spiritual side acts like a compass, reminding us when we are being true to ourselves. Typically people who live consciously with spirit connection and soul purpose understand the world is the way it is so that we can make it better.

In contrast, some of us don't know that by ignoring the voices of our souls and spirits, we are actually depriving ourselves of what makes us unique and special. By allowing ourselves to sacrifice the gifts that would otherwise come from living our true nature, we are in reality holding back from the world just those things we could so powerfully contribute.

The conversation between Socrates and Glaucon from Plato's *The Republic* comes to mind when I think of this choice. In Plato's allegory of the cave, some prisoners are in an underground cave, chained to the wall. The wall in front of them is blank. They have been there for a long time, and they have no memory of life before the cave. One day the door is left open, and light comes in. The prisoners notice shadowy images moving on the wall in front of them. Some prisoners will try to ignore the images and come up with explanations about what they could be. Others will choose to struggle until they can break free of their chains in order to turn around, go toward the light, and see where the images are coming from. This second group of prisoners will eventually find a world of forms they had forgotten existed. Finding their way into the light, they will have the opportunity to experience the true nature of their existence. The remaining prisoners, fearing the light, will choose to stay in the cave, pretending they never saw the images at all.

Who would we choose to be? Would we choose to be one of the prisoners who remains chained in the shadows, safely resigned to that existence. Or would we be the one who walks free and into the light of the sun, able to embrace a better understanding of our self-worth and potential?

The Connection between Your Power and Your Beliefs

Do you want to be powerful? Power comes when you realize that you can only achieve what you believe. Many people are unconscious of how their beliefs are running their lives.

When we blame others, the world, or fate for our shortsightedness or unconscious motives, we let go of taking any responsibility. In doing that, we are essentially giving up our power. We cannot change our lives and solve problems when we give away our power to affect the situation. When we are open to asking ourselves, "What was my part in creating the situation?" we find reasons and understandings that allow us to invent a better outcome. At the very least, the new insight could provide us with an important lesson for next time.

I love it when I can witness my clients emerge from their shadow selves and rediscover (or discover for the first time) true meaning in their lives. When their accurate self-awareness and guiding purposes line up with a vision for a bold new future and any conflicting beliefs have been addressed, I can literally watch them transform into their purposes right before my eyes. When we know our purpose, we are able to formulate a plan to achieve it. The discomfort of breaking through barriers is just a mosquito compared to the power of driving passion and joy. Instead of stumbling along, rapid-fire thinkers can soar into the skies.

In fact, I watched myself transform when I did this work. My life purpose is to be an asset wherever I go. My life purpose has a twofold focus—ending the stigma of ADHD and bettering the lives of animals and their habitats. I want to be a beacon to illuminate the path whether it's about improving the plight of wildlife or ending the negative label ADHD.

When I was growing up, I knew only the anger, disappointment, and pain that resulted from the chaos around me. It required years of therapy, training, and hard work, but I was able to make it out of the shadows and into the light. I will always remember the moment when I sat up in my bed in the middle of the night and said to myself, "I'm an asset. Yes, I am, and I worked very hard to get here." I came to see that for a long time I had been hiding in my work and business to keep from thinking about what I considered the painful questions regarding my life. When I finally realized that I was an asset (rather than a mistake), I discovered my ability to forgive and move on. Healing my past set me free. That's why I believe in the cognitive aspect of coaching. I know that we can change our thinking. We can turn away from negative and self-defeating attitudes and turn toward positive and self-empowering ones. Our life is a mirror of the way we think.

CHAPTER 15

Envisioning Your Destiny

The next step toward a new action plan is to apply visualizing techniques, right attitudes, and positive thinking. In this chapter I will walk you through exercises that will help you embrace the possibility of a future where self-control and unwavering focus bring you accomplishment and happiness.

Once we better understand our lives and ourselves, we find we can let go of blame. We no longer wish things were different. We now have reasons for how things have unfolded in our lives. We can begin to see how our previous experiences were necessary to gain the wisdom we need to evolve into who we have become. Now we can begin to make peace with those reasons and stop blaming our parents, others, and ourselves.

Now we are going to take the understandings and tools we have gained from our insights and use them all to empower us. We will use them to make a plan for our future based on confidence in our inherent strengths and abilities.

It's vitally important to take a break here to talk about how having an innovator brain has affected the plans you have for your life. Most of us get so used to living in a bubble of comfort, protection, and resignation that we no longer think about the dreams and intentions we once had for ourselves. We get through the day and feel good that there was not a major mishap. We can pay our bills this month, and we can forget about the problems of tomorrow for another night. But is that all there is and all we really want? What if we knew we were cheating ourselves out of what we really deserved and that we were settling for much less than we had to?

It's a habit we got into when we began to believe that we were flawed and would never be good enough. The habit of trying not to draw attention to ourselves and spending a great deal of energy on managing our behavior caused us to create a belief in our subconscious mind that we must set our sights low. We were taught to remember our deficits and how our disordered minds will always prevent us from achieving great things. Of course, we know that those with this brain type have managed to bring world-changing advancements and critically needed solutions throughout history. Many persevered and rose above the naysayers and detractors, some at great cost to themselves and their reputations. But doesn't every person with an innovator brain deserve the same opportunities as other people?

The way back to becoming who we most want to become in the world, whether we have innovator brains or not, begins with a belief in ourselves and includes the support of others. People with innovator brains need to be taught from a young age how to appreciate their special gifts and how to use their strengths to manage time, tasks, and expectations. The irony of this is that these strategies are fairly easy to put in place with minimal training. However, they do require ongoing support. Innovators will always need help from others. They will need mentoring, coaching, and accountability in order to succeed. And for optimal success, when possible they need to let other people do the things they dislike and are not good at so they can focus on the things they excel at and love to do.

As we learn more about ourselves as innovators, we can use our talents in ways that create opportunities for us. And in order to use our talents, we must learn to overcome old habits and belief systems that no longer serve us. Sometimes we can't see sufficient rewards now and in the future, so we may lack enough motivation to do the work of changing our behavior. For this reason, it is important to set a compelling purpose and vision for our lives so that we have something worth all of the hard work.

The good news is that we all need something to work toward that matters to us. We feel joy and happiness when we are building our lives in ways that contribute to the future so that it's better than the present and will bring us the rewards we hope for. That is why it is so surprising that more of us don't have a distinct vision for the future, the goals that will get us there, and a plan for reaching the goals. When we have a plan to follow, we are more likely to get where we are going in the time frame we want. We are more likely to succeed at our dreams when we have rules to live by and a schedule to follow.

Creating Your Vision

Creating a vision is such an exciting thing to do! When you begin, your whole body tingles. You really realize that you can create what you believe and what you intend. When you can imagine, write down, and then say your vision out loud, you have already come halfway. I'm saying you have already finished fifty percent of what it takes to manifest your vision. Why is this so? It is so because you are telling your subconscious mind that your vision *lives*, that it exists here and now. So as you repeat your vision over and over again, your subconscious mind is getting the message that it is falling behind and needs to catch up. And we know that the subconscious mind is our autopilot, and it is the rich reservoir of what we believe we can accomplish. Thought creates everything. When you focus and employ your soul and spirit energy, then you bring into being what you have conceived of in thought.

When you act like you're doing it now, you actually are doing it now! Here is an example: I wake up in the morning, and I declare that I have three great new clients that love my coaching and are making great strides as a result of working with me. I see these new clients and imagine them as actual people with real stories and real problems. I see them day after day in my mind's eye and feel gratitude for the opportunity to help them at this point in their lives. Then at some point in the near future, clients similar to my description will join my practice. So how can this be? When we are focused, confident, positive, and faithful, visualizing in our minds and believing that we already have what we want, our subconscious mind wants to end the dissonance so it brings our vision to us. The key is to keep repeating your visualization to yourself and out loud. Although we cannot predict exactly when our gifts will come, they always do.

"I want to help women who suffer from domestic violence" is not a vision. However lofty and heart felt, this is not a cause someone can sign on to. It is stated as a desire instead of a commitment, it is not specific about how it will be done, and it lacks enthusiasm. It also lacks an outcome. The subconscious mind doesn't understand past and future, only the present. So how can you make this a vision statement? Here are two examples: "I am a member of an organization that strives to help women and children avoid the pain and tragedy of domestic violence through public education and the establishment of safe houses." Or you could also say, "I am someone who cares deeply about healing family relationships, and I work hard to enable people to live as whole and healthy human beings through my work as a social worker". Let's say one of these statements was your vision, what could have been your statement of purpose? Consider the following statement: "My purpose is to bring the issue of domestic violence out into the open so I can raise awareness of the issue within the community. I do this by educating people through seminars and collaborations with mental health professionals. I engage with women and men in groups and individually, exploring this topic and the pain and dysfunction that domestic violence causes. In order to fulfill my vision, I also create mental health support centers where children and adults can go for help." This is one case in point. If you don't have a vision, ask yourself what ideal or conviction motivates you and fits your sense of purpose. What higher meaning have you been looking for in life?

Sometimes people need to take an extra step. A vision isn't enough. They need a mission. A mission is a large call to action that usually involves other people and solves a larger problem. Missions could include things like ending hunger in your community, developing an organization that raises money to house the homeless, or creating an international organization to work for world justice.

The process we have been talking about is hard to accomplish on your own. It requires a second person to work through the issues that will inevitably arise and may cause you to get stuck in places. And most importantly, your coach or mentor will be the one who shows up to make sure you don't give up on your vision and plan. I want you to see the importance of doing this valuable work. Not having an accurate self-awareness, guiding purpose, and vision for a bold new future is like trying to tie your shoes with one hand. It's extremely difficult. Having the greatest books in the world at your disposal won't matter if you can't read.

As for me, being an asset to everyone I meet, especially to those who have been labeled with ADHD, means that it is my job to do that to the best of my ability. I will not always succeed at this, but my job is to wake up each day with that focus. I am a champion for a healthy planet, especially when it comes to saving wildlife and habitat. I can count on my subconscious mind to aid me as I repeat my awareness, purpose, and vision statements in the morning, throughout the day, and before I go to bed at night.

Pay attention to your thoughts, and you can learn to control them. Observing the results of paying attention to the way you think about things will show you where negative thinking patterns are creating poor results for you and where positive thinking has created good results. Repeatedly visualize the results you will have in your life when you change your way of thinking about things. Keep practicing changing from negative and resigned thinking to positive and empowered thinking, and you will see good results!

I know what it feels like to not hear the directions and feel ashamed you have to ask others to repeat themselves. I know how it feels to be afraid of drawing attention to my incompetence, so I have to struggle to understand on my own without help. At the age of seven, I lived every day in fear of the teacher asking me in front of my classmates to turn right or left and I would be glued to the spot, not knowing which way to turn until someone grabbed my arm. I remember the anxiety I would constantly feel about what instructions or information I had missed that all the other children around me had gotten. I distinctly remember how impossible it was for me to get my homework done. I lived in dread that I would have to endure the teacher's disapproval and the disapproving looks from my classmates when I was asked where the assignment was and I had to publicly state I didn't have it. I remember how it felt to be stupid and completely incompetent.

None of us want our children to grow up with such pain and shame. And all of us deserve another chance to learn how to create a future we love and can be proud of for ourselves and for our children. So now we are going to put it all together so that you can live the way you were meant to before the stigma of ADHD made you stop trying to achieve your dreams.

CHAPTER 16

Mapping Your Future

It is time to combine your new self-awareness, guiding purpose, and future vision into a carefully designed strategic plan. Using the following formula and five-step process, you will learn how to create a realistic framework you can use to reach your goals and achieve your vision.

Creating a Blueprint in Five Steps

Step 1: Accurate Self-Awareness

Our self-awareness is built on understanding and accepting who we are and what we stand for. It's our strong suit, and it's what makes us special and unique. It's the gift of self-appreciation that we are happy to pass on to others. Self-awareness comes from removing unconscious blocks and self-doubt from our minds through listening to feedback from therapists, counselors, coaches, friends, or associates. Without feedback from professionals and others in our lives, we can remain blind to what is holding us back from being happy, satisfied people. We humans are prone to blind spots. We don't always understand why our relationships don't work and why we're not living the lives we once believed in. Our tendency is to inaccurately blame these instances on others or ourselves instead of enlisting feedback from people we trust so that we can change the problem behaviors and get on with life.

For your self-awareness step, after you have utilized the previous suggestions about how to clear your blocks and self-doubts, write a positive and uplifting statement about who you are based on the real truth you have uncovered about yourself.

- I am someone who knows the secrets behind being a first-class _____.
- I am someone who has worked hard and is proud to excel at buying houses, using a computer, being an engineer, cooking _____.
- I am someone who makes a significant difference in the lives of others through healing, working to solve homelessness, doing my part to save the environment, and _____.
- I am someone with the special ability to bring people together _____.
- I'm an asset.

Step 2: Guiding Purpose

Now it is time to choose your purpose. Don't worry if it you make a choice and then change your mind. Sometimes that happens because we are able to discover our true focus after we have started with another one. Just write down what is true for you now. Embellish it with adjectives and descriptions that make it feel even more powerful and compelling when you read it. Spend a week with the statement. Make it sound and feel just the way you want it. Consider the following examples:

- "My purpose is to create an organization that ensures every child in my community has enough food to eat."
- "My purpose is to constantly improve my family's standard of living and create a surplus of money in our lives."
- "My purpose is to live debt free."
- "My purpose is to achieve happiness for myself and my family through building strong, loving relationships."
- "My purpose is to save as many elephants from the ivory trade as I can."
- "My purpose is to be happy and to spread happiness."

Step 3: Bold New Future

The next step is to create your bold new future. Your vision for your future will be the reasons and motivation behind your purpose and where you want your purpose to take you in the future. Why did you create that particular purpose? What is the vision you are here to achieve in your lifetime that comes from your purpose? What special gift or talent do you want to share with the world that is uniquely yours? Here are some examples:

- "My vision is that I do my part to save the North Atlantic right whale from extinction."
- "My vision is that I work toward ending domestic violence for all women, particularly Latina women and women of color."
- "My vision is that I live with courage, keep my home a sanctuary, love and support my family, and have financial security."

Step 4: Composed Plan

Once you have your purpose and vision for a bold new future, you are ready to plan four time frames: six months, one year, two years, and finally four or five years. The six-months plan will help you remain focused by giving you the benefit of having measurable accomplishments and more immediate results. The twelve-months plan will allow you to capture the longer-term picture of what you are able to realistically accomplish in a year. The two-year plan makes sure you stay focused on the long-term picture that you are working to achieve and will keep you certain of the progress you are making. And your four- to five-year plan helps you wrap your hands and head around what you need to consistently accomplish if you're going to meet your goals and achieve your future vision within your expected time frame. All steps are important components for keeping you focused and motivated and benchmarking your progress. Each plan needs to be a constant reminder of what you are up to daily, weekly, monthly, and yearly and how things need to play out if you are going to stay motivated when times are rough.

The best way for you to get started on your future plan is to purchase a two-year calendar or two separate yearly calendars. The following is my five-step process, which will be the backbone of your future plan:

1. Record in the calendar the completion date you are hoping for. Do not be afraid to pick a date or worry about whether you will have it all done by then. Having a deadline or delivery date means you are going to get much closer than you would have without one.

2. Begin your planning by working backward. Working backward will allow you to come up with or invent the steps you will need to meet your goals and deadlines. Do not concern yourself with whether they are the best steps or

are adequate for success. Just brainstorm and make a good start. You can always revise as you go along.

3. As you work backward, imagine the tasks you will need to accomplish and the actions you will need to take if you are going to achieve your plan. Making adjustments and actually perfecting your plan comes later. The first step is to tap your brain and create a skeleton plan.

4. Initially you will write down all the ideas that come to mind. For this reason, it is a good idea to purchase a monthly poster-sized calendar to hang on the wall in your planning space. You can tear off the months and hang them in a sequence so the full six months or year is viewable. You can create a color-coded system by using different sizes of sticky notes, highlighters, and markers. Using sticky notes and erasable writing implements will allow you to make necessary changes at the beginning of your design process. Having a vertical constant reminder of what you can look forward to in your future will keep you excited and confident and help you maintain consistency with the planning process.

Step 5: Support System

Bring in a coach or similar mentor to hold you accountable and help you stay focused on your plan, executing the actions necessary to move forward. My experience has taught me that without the help of someone to hold them to a standard of consistent progress, most people are more likely to struggle to achieve progress.

As you embrace your new plan, there will be critical times when you are vulnerable to being thrown off course. Don't allow your dream to wither on the vine. Get help from someone experienced in working with people who are moving to another stage in their lives and need someone to hold them to a well-thought-out plan. In the beginning when we are starting something new, we are more vulnerable to things like losing interest, getting lost in the process, finding it all too difficult and cumbersome, and becoming confused. This can cause us to just give up and wonder why we ever thought we could accomplish such a massive goal. Without the support of at least one committed person to hold us to our dream, we could lose it. Make sure you don't take these risks. Enlist the help of someone who is committed to holding you accountable. You will especially need this person at the times you are considering abandoning your vision.

Creating your Blueprint

The Question of "Are You Ready?"

Being able to emotionally face the truth about yourself—that truth about why you continue to tolerate the painful circumstances in your life—is a necessary ingredient to creating your blueprint. Being ready is a big deal. Experiences and ideas will merge into important insights when you're ready. When you are ready, you are willing to stop suffering and struggling and have faith in yourself. Being ready means you commit to adhering to your plan and support system and never give up no matter how many times you fall off track. Remember that mistakes are only opportunities to learn and grow. Believing in yourself and taking advantage of what life has to offer you is priceless.

Consider the following six questions you should ask yourself to determine if you are ready to move forward to a bold new future.

- How satisfied are you with the life you have created for yourself so far?

- How would you change your life to make it one you truly hunger for?
- What will be possible for you and your life if you make these changes?
- What are you willing to do to get a better understanding of what is holding you back from making these changes?
- How can you use these understandings to bust through the wall of fear that is holding you back?
- What are you willing to give up in order to have this new life you are starving for?
- What are you waiting for?

Reviewing the Steps to Achieving a Bold Vision

- Get clear about who you are (self-image), where you're going (guiding purpose), and how you conceive of your bold new future (vision).
- Create your six-month, twelve-month, two-year, and four- to five-year plans, working backward from your completion date.
- Get help from a coach or mentor you feel makes the grade.
- Meditate regularly about your future.
- Contemplate your new future by visualizing yourself already there.
- Get comfortable being uncomfortable with your vision. Remember, you are stepping out of your comfort zone.
- Never give up.
- Again, get the kind of help that ensures you cannot fail.

If you stick with it through the ups and downs, confusion and clarity, failures and successes, falling off track more times than you can count and getting back on again, the light will eventually come on. It might creep up on you like the dawn, or it might simply switch on in a second. The key is to believe in *yourself* enough to try.

Aligning with a New Life Blueprint

Hope for a better life for ourselves and those we care about can be part of our future. When we take the time to plan, set goals, and measure them, we are working toward a vision of our life as it could be. When we let our life go whichever way the wind is blowing, there is no way to predict what course our future will take. In this section you will learn how to create a blueprint for where you want to go, beginning with where you are right now. You will create the steps and actions you need to take and the habits you need to develop to live the rewarding and satisfying life you were meant for.

Here is a quote for you to repeat to help you acknowledge yourself and your innovator brain: "When I can celebrate and truly own what makes me different, I will be able to tap into the source of my creative power."

Marilyn's Story

A thirty-eight-year-old woman named Marilyn came to me five years ago for an appointment. Then she left and did not come back to see me until two years later. When she came back, she said, "I think I'm ready for you now. I have the same problem now I had two years ago. I have no meaning in my life. My children are gone, and I'm separated from my husband. Although we're trying to get back together, I just don't seem to care anymore."

I began our work together by urging Marilyn to take a look at her own thinking and to examine what she believed about herself. We inventoried her beliefs about what she thought she was capable of. We quickly discovered she had no idea because she had closed herself off from her own needs and was in the habit of attending only to the needs of others. She reported her husband was controlling and manipulative, and she had given her complete attention to her sons since they were born. She couldn't remember the last time she thought of her future or how she felt about her life.

Gradually Marilyn began to step back from her lockstep existence and see the bigger picture. She looked at her life as one would look at a map. She recognized the patterns in her thinking and how they had led her to where she stood now. From this vantage point, Marilyn and I sketched a plan so she could begin doing things that made her happy. But first we had to cover some important ground so that she could reconnect to herself because Marilyn was unable to identify what made her happy at that point. Being numb to her own feelings had made Marilyn a stranger to herself.

After she came up with some ideas that might make her happy, Marilyn had to face the fact that she had become afraid to do almost anything. For a long time, she had been a passive responder to others. It took a while for her to learn to take tiny steps and try new things. To assist in her progress, each time Marilyn ventured out and tried something new that she enjoyed, we would go over the experience together afterward as evidence of her ability to know herself and find out what contributed to her happiness.

Each time a bigger step was required, Marilyn would retreat back into the shadows. But because she had me as her coach, she kept at it, and after a number of months, she was able to say with some confidence that she wanted to volunteer to do something important. She said, "I thought I would need to be paid to feel valuable, but now I don't think so. I feel I may be happy working to benefit others without the expectation of compensation."

Marilyn discovered she had a passion for ending childhood obesity. Through volunteering, she also found she had a gift for raising funds for schools and community organizations. As she began to talk to her friends and people who knew her, she thought of combining her passion for helping overweight children and her gift for fundraising. She volunteered for and soon was being paid to create programs for local schools in her community.

Marilyn had discovered fulfillment and purpose. She told me that the difference between her life before she found her purpose and her life after she discovered her passion was like going from feeling dead to feeling fully alive. For Marilyn, that was quite a statement to make!

The things most important to Marilyn were relationships, health, contribution, and justice. Marilyn's accurate self-awareness statement said, "I am a passionate advocate who cares deeply for the physical health and well-being of others, especially helping my family and children everywhere achieve healthy bodies and minds." Marilyn's guiding purpose statement said, "My purpose is to raise funds for schools and community organizations in order to confront the problem of childhood obesity and ensure all children have healthy diets and healthy lives." Marilyn's vision statement for her bold new future said, "I bring education and funding to parents and children, schools and community organizations across the country to realize the goal of raising children who exercise regularly and eat healthy."

Marilyn was on a mission. It began with the simple statement and eventually grew from one page and ten steps to a hundred-page, ten-year plan showing affiliations, groups, budgets, and targeted demographics across the country.

There were times when I didn't know whether or not Marilyn would make it. It was slow going because she had to get to know her real and competent self all over again. We were changing Marilyn's passivity into initiative while helping her come to terms with a cripplingly low self-esteem. How did she do it? She just wouldn't quit. Marilyn described it this way: Fear climbed up out of her gut and choked her in the night, and self-hatred crawled out of her thoughts and shot her between the eyes. Marilyn just would not and could not give up. Week after week and month after month, she slogged through her fears and failures and steeled her faith. She believed she could do it even when she was screaming inside to give up because she didn't think she had what it took to succeed.

When she thought, *What's wrong with me?* Marilyn got into the habit of saying to herself, "Marilyn, the only thing wrong with you is that you keep asking that question. You are strong. You are smart. Your life stands for something."

Every morning and night, Marilyn sat still in meditation, going inward and connecting with positive messages from her authentic self and the truth about who she really was. She listened with her heart even when it felt uncomfortable, even when her impulsivity and distractibility were insisting that she begin all those things she had to do that day. Marilyn stayed put, and it paid off.

This is the life that Marilyn, who started out empty and hopeless, was finally able to embrace. Tears come to my eyes as I write this. This is courage. This is truly a testament to the power of refusing to quit until you find meaning and purpose for your life. This is you. This is me. This is all of us. And this is also the power of ADHD coaching.

CHAPTER 17

The Importance of Ongoing Healing

Each of us deserves to exist, to be successful, and to be loved for who we truly are. When individuals discover that they are sending their own brain messages about being stupid, incompetent, and unlovable because of their perceived shortcomings, they are continually paving the road ahead for more of the same. Remember, we achieve what we believe. Marilyn's Mount Everest was to change her ill-conceived beliefs about herself from dysfunction into ability, disorder into competence, and deficit into skills and talents. Looking back, I think Marilyn would tell you it was worth the struggle.

Like Marilyn, in order to learn to reinterpret the meaning of negative past events and free ourselves from their influences, we must first share painful, embarrassing, or traumatic memories. This procedure involves engaging in a process of reinterpreting and redefining past events wherever the pain and blame still linger.

The following are some possible steps you can take to work on this issue. Remember that transformation is more likely to take place when you do it out loud in privacy with a trusted person.

- Consider what meaning you derived from a painful event or situation in the past.

- Ask yourself for another interpretations of this painful event from a positive, self-affirming perspective where it becomes an important and necessary learning experience for you.

- Consider how over time your initial self-incriminating interpretation of the event has contributed to negative thoughts and outlooks.

- Investigate the possibility that an inaccurate understanding of this past event has been robbing you of self-worth. A new and more believable version of the event, based on your current understanding, can now be invented. Was it truly your fault? Based on your knowledge at the time, could there have been any other outcome? Do bad things happen to good people?

- Finally, ask yourself which interpretation—since it is only an interpretation after all—you would rather have contributing to your life. The historical one you've been suffering from or the new positive, self-affirming one you just created?

Armed with a new understanding of the past event and your role in it and freed from the past negative story you made up, there is now room for your innovative mind to change the memory of the event and take back this piece of your self-worth.

Sharon's Story

Here is an example of this process: Sharon's mother verbally and physically abused her until she left home at the age of sixteen. Because this abuse began when she was a very young child who was vulnerable and dependent, Sharon only thought that she was so disappointing to her mother that her mother was willing to hurt her over and over again. When I met her, Sharon was battling depression.

She did not have an intimate partner, and she had bounced from job to job with no financial or career stability. On top of that, Sharon had been diagnosed with ADHD, and she was trying to understand how it had affected her over time.

With the help of ADHD coaching, Sharon was finally able to see how this earliest interpretation of her unworthiness had affected her life, making relationships very difficult for her and trust nearly impossible. She then worked on reinterpreting her childhood from a different perspective: that as a very young child, she could not be guilty of being a disappointment. Instead, the truth was she had never gotten the love and reassurance all children need to grow up confident and self assured. Under those circumstances, how could she be expected to have a healthy self-image and develop trust?

Sharon created a new interpretation of her past based on the possibility that she was a worthy and talented person who had been dealt a difficult hand. She admitted she did not know what she was capable of, but she was interested in finding out. She started to notice that her childhood may have robbed her of love and confidence in herself, but she had a level of understanding and compassion for other people who had led painful lives. Sharon began working with emotionally handicapped children and abandoned animals. She found she had a gift for deep and profound healing that she may not have had if her upbringing had been different. She realized her unique gift to heal children, animals, and addicts gave her great happiness, and she was able to build a life around these unique capabilities that was both financially and personally rewarding.

When we think we are the problem, there is no hope. When we realize we have the tools to change our perception and interpretation of painful events from our past, freeing ourselves from an interpretation that never served us in any positive and fair way, we are no longer victims. Then we become powerful people who are able to contribute to ourselves and others with an abundance of hope and possibility.

Esther's Story

I am currently working with Esther, a young innovator who has been the victim of her husband's verbal abuse for years. Through our work together, we are trying to figure out why Esther has allowed the abuse to continue for so long.

We began our work with the lessons growing up that Esther learned about herself that may have caused her to think that this is what she has to endure. Is she fearful of abandonment? Is she worried she can't make it on her own? Does she believe she deserves this treatment? She says she has been avoiding this conversation with herself for a long time, but now she's hoping to change that. Esther is beginning to realize from our conversations the damage her reluctance to stand up for herself is doing to herself and her children.

Three months have come and gone, and Esther has begun to find the strength to accept the truth about herself and her situation. Her husband is unlikely to change, and there is always the risk that things will escalate into physical abuse. Additionally, she has become even more painfully aware of the bad example she is setting for her children. With my support, Esther has begun to explore ideas and make plans. She appears very committed, and I don't think she's going to back down. When Esther has moved away from her husband and is settled again with her children in a healthy environment, she plans to rebuild her life with a determined focus and all the self-confidence she can muster for the hard work ahead. I believe in Esther's ability to start a new life, and I hope to be with her every step of the way.

CHAPTER 18

Final Thoughts

The most important way to free ourselves from the ADHD stigma is to realize that our strengths far outweigh our limitations. It is critical that that we not let the pain of the past hold us back from the possibilities of the future. I believe that every member of the ADHD—I mean, innovator brain—community has valuable contributions to offer their families, communities, and the economy. I'm hoping that after you have read this book, if you didn't before, you will agree with me now.

The first step in healing our past and embracing our future is understanding our emotional response to growing up with ADHD, which we now know is more accurately described as our innovator brain. We also need to understand how it has harmed our ability to believe in ourselves and how we perform in life. To do the important work of understanding our innovative brain type, we must also be willing to do the healing work. One cannot move forward without the other. As we heal, we open up the doors to using our innovative strengths to accomplish and succeed in our careers, personal lives, and relationships.

Your Innovator Brain – The Truth About ADHD

So how do we open those doors? First we need help because we cannot do it alone.

We need to find someone we can trust and not settle for the first person or professional that comes along. The strategy of using parents, friends, or others without professional status has been known to have limited results in the long run, and it might also present other problems along the way. It is best to hire a professional ADHD coach we have faith in. When a relationship has the potential to impact who we can be and what we can accomplish in our lives as we move forward, it is important to choose the right person.

Once you have chosen that person, you will develop the type of relationship where you can be 100 percent truthful with them at all times about what is really going on and how you honestly feel. This way, you will get the most from the coaching, and it will allow you to change certain behaviors and reach your goals. You will also need to put your coaching relationship at the top of your priority list. After all, your own personal transformation from attention deficit disorder to bright and capable innovator is no small thing!

When we go back and explore the history of our understanding of this brain type, we can see a pattern of misunderstanding from the beginning. Mistakes were made initially in our understanding of the innovator brain type before we had the science and knew how to accurately explain the situation. It's time to set the record straight. It's time to look at the innovator brain for what it is in application—a specific brain type that includes the exceptional ability to innovate, a brain type with a nonlinear way of doing things, a brain that's perfect for discovering the theory of relativity, the electric light bulb, the polio vaccine, and a cure for cancer one day.

Your new and most important job is to appreciate your brain for what it is. It's the best asset you will ever have, and that includes all the behaviors that go with it. There is no way to give you the creative brilliance that comes natural to you without the behaviors that cause you difficulty (e.g., disorganization, distractibility, and emotional turmoil). You have the capacity to learn to develop new habits and strategies that will enable you to get better at working with all of these, but your innate and exceptional curiosity, creativity and problem solving skills cannot be taught. That's your potential whether you use it or not.

Getting to know your brain better involves learning to appreciate your strengths and weaknesses and remembering what you need in order to function successfully. Once you've learned to understand yourself as an innovator brain type, you will be able to develop the confidence to advocate for yourself in all types of situations. That way, you can make your unique contribution with strength and courage. This is what I want for all of us. It is about time we stopped calling ourselves disordered and distracted and moved on to the truth of being capable and gifted. It's time to leave the past behind and move on to what we're all capable of.

WORKS CITED

Akhtar, S. and M.K. O'Neil. 2013. On Freud's "The Unconscious." London: Karnac Books.

Archer, D. 2014. "ADHD: The Entrepreneur's Superpower." Forbes, May 14. http://www.forbes.com/sites/dalearcher/2014/05/14/adhd-the-entrepreneurs-superpower/

Byrne, P. 2001. "Psychiatric Stigma." The British Journal of Psychiatry 178(3): 281-284.

Consumer Reports Best Buy Drugs. 2012. Evaluating Prescription Drugs Used to Treat: Attention-Deficit/Hyperactivity Disorder (ADHD). Consumers Union of U.S., Inc. http://www.consumerreports.org/cro/2012/03/best-treatments-for-children-with-adhd/index.htm

Corrigan, P. and D.L. Penn. 1999. "Lessons from Social Psychology on Discrediting Psychiatric Stigma." American Psychologist 54: 765-776

DellaContrada, J. 2005. "Medication Combined with Behavior Therapy Works Best for ADHD Children, Study Finds." University at Buffalo Study for Treatments of Children with Attention Deficit

Hyperactivity Disorder (ADHD), May 5. http://www.buffalo.edu/news/releases/2005/05/7280.html

Dyer, W. 2005. The Power of Intention. New York: Hay House.

Griffin, R. "What's the Difference between ADD and ADHD?" Understood for Learning and Attention Issues website. Accessed 3 November 2015. http://www.ncld.org/types-learning-disabilities/adhd-related-issues/adhd/difference-between-add-adhd

Hayward, P. and J. Bright. 1997. "Stigma and Mental Illness: a Review and Critique." Journal of Mental Health 6: 345-354.

Holland, K. and V. Higuera. "The History of ADHD: A Timeline." Accessed 3 November 2015. http://www.healthline.com/health/adhd/history #Overview1

Isaacson, W. 2015. The Innovators – How a Group of Hackers, Geniuses, and Geeks Created the Digital Revolution. New York: Simon and Schuster.

Jitahidi, J. 2004. Intuitive Management: Creating an Inspired Workforce. Maryland: Publish America.

Klein, R. G., S. Mannuzza, M.A. Olazagasti, E. Roizen, J.A. Hutchison, E.C. Lashua, F.X. Castellanos. 2012. "Clinical and Functional Outcome of Childhood Attention-Deficit/Hyperactivity Disorder 33 Years Later." Archives in General Psychiatry 69(12): 1295-1303.

McCarthy, L. F. "Top Ten Questions About Medications for Children with ADHD ... Answered!" Accessed 3 November 2015. http://www.additudemag.com/adhd/article/1592.html

Mooers Montana, G. "Identities." Accessed 3 November 2015. a http://www.oneminuteu.com/default.taf?sort_by=&page= search&search_q=IDENTITIES&zipcode=Zipcode

National Institute of Mental Health. 1999, Revised 2009. The Multimodal Treatment of Attention Deficit Hyperactivity Disorder Study (MTA): Questions and Answers. http://www.nimh.nih. gov/funding/clinical-research/practical/mta/the-multimodal-treatment-of attention-deficit-hyperactivity-disorder-study-mta-questions-and-answers.shtml

Quily, P. 2006. "Top Ten Advantages of ADHD in a High Tech Career." Adult ADD Strengths blog. http://www.adultaddstrengths. com /2006/02/09/top-10-advantages-of-add-in-a-high-tech-career/

Sayce, L. 2000. Psychiatric Patient to Citizen. London: MacMillan.

Schlosberg, A. 1993. "Psychiatric Stigma and Mental Health Professionals (Stigmatizers and Destigmatizers)." Medicine and Law 12: 409-416

Still, Sir George Frederick. 1902. Some Abnormal Psychical Conditions in Children: the Goulstonian Lectures. The Lancet 1:1008-1012.

Stroh, Madeline P. 2011. "Bradley's Benzedrine Studies in Children with Behavioral Disorders." Yale Journal of Biology and Medicine 84(1): 27-33.

Wake Forest Baptist Medical Center. "Long-term ADHD Drug Use Appears Safe." http://www. wakehealth.edu/News-Releases/2012/ Long-term_ADHD_Drug_Use_ Appears_Safe.htm

Wikipedia. "Augusta Ada King, Countess of Lovelace." Accessed 3 November 2015. https://www.en.wikipedia.org/wiki/Ada_Lovelace

Wolff, J. "Is ADHD a Positive Force for Writers and Others?" Time to Write: Jurgen Wolff blog. Accessed 3 November 2015. http://timetowrite.blogs.com/weblog/2010/06/is-adhd-a-positive-force-for-writers-and-others.

Wundt, W. 1902. Principles of Physiological Psychology. http://www.psychclassics.yorku.ca/Wundt/Physio/